DAVID

CHOSEN BY GOD

By Daryl T Sanders

Author's web site is found at www.booksbydaryl.com
Author's blog http://blog.booksbydaryl.com/
Author's email 12dsanders@gmail.com

Other books by Daryl T Sanders are:

God the Father

Peter Finds Life (Peter in the gospels)

Peter Finds Power (Peter in the book of Acts)

Peter Finds Purpose (Peter in the epistles)

WHY – **Questions along life's journey**

Finding the Power to Heal

All Bible references used the New King James Version as found on the web site www.blueletterbible.org. Definitions used are from Strong's Concordance or Vine's

The underlines of words in scripture and those words put in bold were at the writer's discretion for purposes of the author's emphasis.

Big thanks to my new friend Renny Severance for advice, editing gift and golfing buddy. I write like I talk and Renny helped as much as he could.

PROLOGUE

In 1978 on Siesta Key Florida, I wanted to spend my personal Bible study time on David during our family vacation. No man in the Bible has more content on his complete life than David. So I decided to keep track of all decision points in his life and examine his life in detail. I still have those yellow legal pages where I wrote down all those key scriptures and kept my observations. Over the years I have taught on David and have thought about David.

Two years ago I took note that David's name is in the Bible more than the name of Jesus. David's name appears in the Bible 1139 times in 968 verses and Jesus' name appears 983 times in 942 verses.

In fact, it is amazing that Jesus chose to use the name of David as a reference or an identifier to who He was while on earth. Since He chose David above all other men then I wanted to try to discover why.

In the New Testament we are told that "David was a man after God's own heart." I pray I have captured some of the reasons that God would so measure the man David. Obviously his life had its shortcomings but yet he was a king that built the nation of Israel to a worldwide power. He built an army that had no equal. His disciplined soldiers and battle strategies were ahead of his time.

In the last half of his rule, he devised a twice daily worship service, wrote hundreds of songs, built thousands of instruments, hired full time singers and dancers, and designed the most magnificent building ever built on earth.

Was it these achievements or was it something else? What did his heart have to do with these achievements?

Every event in this book is in the Bible. But the thoughts expressed in the book are my interpolations of what could have been going on in the hearts and minds of the people involved.

I dedicate this book to my wife, Barbara Taylor Sanders – who saved my life in helping me and our children reconnect with our Lord and Savior Jesus Christ.

Cover design by Robert "Bo" Sanders.

CHAPTER ONE

It was a moonless night; the stars were shining between the drifting clouds. Each breath, shepherd or sheep, escaped like a puff of smoke. The chill in the air was common this time of year. The ten year old shepherd boy had been leading his father's sheep for almost two years now. He was on a hill a day's journey from home. The closer winter came the farther from home he led the sheep to find good pasture. He was away from home weeks at a time this time of year. His seven older brothers had all paid their dues taking care of the sheep and now it was his turn.

It was a miracle to his mother that he was even born. His youngest brother was five years older than he and she had thought her day of bearing children was over. After his first six months of tending sheep with his brother he was told he was ready to do it by himself and he didn't mind, he was a dreamer. The stars gave him much to dream majestic thoughts of greatness and grandeur.

The shepherd boy was beautiful. He joined with a half dozen other shepherds from the Bethlehem village and they combined their sheep together. It often amazed him how the sheep knew the voice of their own shepherd and when it was time to return, all a shepherd had to do was call out his own signal and his sheep separated and followed.

They took turns at night sleeping and keeping watch over the flocks. One night around midnight David felt a stirring in his soul. Even at ten years of age, he knew deep in his heart that Yahweh (God of heaven) was real. As he looked out over the heavenly wonders of lights shining from distances unfathomable, David knew in his heart that there was a plan and a purpose to life. Heady thoughts to be sure for a little shepherd boy.

Over his shoulder David slung a chordophone, a small hand-held harp. He had taught himself to play in the long, lonely hours of a shepherd's life. The other shepherds were stationed around the flocks so, other than evening when they ate their evening meal together after the flocks were secured, they were left to their own thoughts.

The thoughts of a dreamer are special. He had heard the stories of Abraham who was a prosperous man living in the major city of the day, Ur of the Chaldees. He knew Yahweh and one day Yahweh told him to pull up stakes and go to a land that Yahweh would show him. This obedience verified that Abraham was a man who lived by faith. To the succeeding generations of the children of Israel he would be known as "the Father of Faith."

Abraham had travelled hundreds of miles to this very land promised him by Yahweh. Abraham was also known as a "Friend of Yahweh." When he first heard this, David puzzled, "What kind of God is this that calls a man a friend?"

David took pride in the fact that Abraham was a distant father to him as well as the father of the entire Nation of Israel. David loved the stories that his own father Jesse told at the feast times about those that came before them.

David began to imagine what it was like to be a man that believed that God would do everything that He promised. God promised Abraham land and he got land. God promised him a son and, although it took many years, Abraham got a son whom he named Isaac. God promised him a family which would cover the earth and there were twelve tribes of people, all from the loins of Abraham.

So this shepherd boy could dream big things because the family before him believed in their God and that their God fulfilled His every promise. David had met many of the people of the other tribes at special feast times every year. He had not met them all by any means, but he already had many friends among his cousins.

Among them was a man known as a prophet of God to all the tribes. His name was Samuel and everyone was fearful whenever Samuel came around because he spoke for God. Imagine someone so close to God that he heard God's words and repeated them!

Samuel would travel around so that each tribe could come and meet with him, but usually only the elders of the tribes went to those meetings. Jesse had told the family that when Samuel spoke it sounded like heaven must sound. The words of Samuel were words that did not go to the minds of the listeners but to their hearts. David did not know what that meant, but he knew there was something great about all of this. And he knew he was a part of it!

One night as he lay dreaming lofty thoughts in his young mind, he heard a noise. The sheep were bedded down for the night and the noise was a low growl. He jumped up because he knew the sound of a predator. Sheep could not defend themselves and were as vulnerable as little babies. David pulled his sling from his belt. He reached into his bag and loaded a stone about a small finger in diameter. It was amazing the speed and power unleashed in a stone that small. David could already sling accurately over three hundred paces. His oldest brother, Eliab, could sling one six hundred paces and was the talk of the tribe.

David heard the sheep bleat about a stone's throw to his left. He walked quietly closer to identify the predator. The darkness hid the shadows, suddenly a twig cracked.

There it was shuffling low to the ground. It was a hungry looking mother bear looking for food for her cubs and herself. David did not sympathize with her needs; he knew that his family could not take the loss of one sheep for they were not wealthy and had many mouths to feed.

She suddenly stopped and lay there waiting for the right moment. Meanwhile David was creeping closer to get a clear shot. He knew he had to hit her in the head. Hitting her in the side would only enrage her and she would come after him.

She began to shuffle closer and was seemingly ready to lunge. David rose and twirled the sling three times around his head to get momentum, he let it fly. The bear fell to the ground dead. David yelled in victory waking up all the other shepherds. Sound travels far in the hills at night. They began yelling back – "what happened?" David broke out in song that he had killed the mother bear and was so excited he jumped and danced as if he were king of the world.

David ran over to the body of the victim. He marveled at the force and power he felt as he knelt down next to her. She was beautiful and she was huge, probably weighing ten times more than he did. His thoughts turned to gratitude; he just knew that Yahweh had been with him. Instead of thinking that he had done it all himself, his thoughts attributed inspiration from God as the reason for success. He viewed Yahweh as his guide and partner. He felt love and care from Yahweh so that his every action was a cooperative effort with God in his own mind and imagination.

His fellow shepherds rushed over with celebration. Who knew what sheep could have been lost? They marveled at their young friend. He was by far the youngest of the group. Yet they all knew he was special. His songs that they heard every night, his constant practicing with his sling and now his killing this bear elevated him in their eyes. Each wondered what they would have done under the same circumstances. After all, what if the bear had turned on him? There were probably three hundred sheep altogether and she would have only taken a couple at most, all good reasons for keeping quiet and hoping she got her business done quickly and left.

After the commotion settled and the skittish sheep were quiet again, David and two of his best friends sat together too excited to sleep. Hushai was about fifteen years old and looked at David like a little brother on one hand and yet as an equal on the other. He could not get over the amazing event that had just taken place. He knew that not one of the other shepherds would have done such a thing. While they were all good with a sling, you would only have one chance from that distance to get off a kill shot.

Abishai, another shepherd about three years older, was scolding David with a smile on his face for taking such a risk. "David, your life is worth much more than a couple of sheep. We would have all shared the loss equally, so why take such a chance?"

David replied, "As I walk these hills with these sheep I have a responsibility for taking care of them. I did not stop to think about what I was doing, I just did it.

"Actually, for about the last six months I have been wondering what I would do if a bear or a lion attacked my sheep. I began imagining how long it would take me to see the predator, draw and load my sling, and let it fly. I got it down with practice to a three count. I knew the key was to decide before one of them showed up.

"So for months now I have looked, loaded and slung about a thousand times, shooting at a bush and pretending it was a bear or a wolf. I began praying for courage to do it if the time ever came. I gained confidence in God and was ready for this day!"

Abishai sat there thinking, "What kind of a boy is this who at such a young age has the thoughts of a warrior? Wait 'til I tell my older brother Joab what happened here today. He is the one I always thought was the warrior of all warriors, but David may be his equal or more."

Hushai sat thinking, "I wonder if David and I will be friends after he becomes great?"

David remained quiet and allowed his heart rate to slow down and come to peace and rest. Both Hushai and Abishai sat knowing that they were in the presence of greatness yet to come.

CHAPTER TWO

Many years earlier, in a place called Mt. Ephraim, there was a man with two wives. His name was Elkanah and one wife was named Hannah and the other named Peninnah. There was fierce competition between the two women that was a constant source of irritation within the tent.

Peninnah got pregnant seemingly every time she was with Elkanah. Hannah on the other hand was barren. Hannah knew in her heart that for some reason Yahweh was withholding a child from her. But Elkanah had a special love for Hannah and all this did was stoke the fires of jealousy in Peninnah.

In Shiloh, a village about a day's journey away, there was a place called the "House of the Lord." There was a priest there by the name of Eli and once each year Elkanah and his two wives went to the House of the Lord to celebrate Passover. Passover was a special remembrance from when all the tribes of Israel were slaves in Egypt. God was ready to have them set free with Moses leading the way.

But Pharaoh did not want to let them go. So God spoke to Moses and told him that every family should slay an unblemished lamb and take the blood of that lamb and paint the doorway to every home. Then, when God sent the "death angel," only those homes with the blood on the doorposts would be "passed over" and in every other home the first born would be killed.

This tragic judgment upon Egypt came after nine other miraculous attacks on this nation. Yahweh brought judgment against everything that the nation of Egypt worshipped. It all started with having Moses lift his staff over the Nile and turning the waters of the Nile to blood and thus killing every fish and serpent that lived in the river. From there the land was overrun with frogs, lice, flies, boils, cattle dying, hail storms, a plague, locusts, and a darkness that no one could see an arm's length. Each one of these was a tragedy in itself but altogether devastating to the great nation of Egypt.

After striking down of the firstborn in every home of the Egyptians including the home of Pharaoh he was finally motivated to set the children of Israel free. Every year after this deliverance the Children of Israel celebrate this great event. For it was not a war to get them free, it was clearly the work of Yahweh that set them free from generations of slavery.

As Elkanah's family set up their temporary tent in Shiloh and were getting things organized, Hannah disappeared. She slipped over to the House of the Lord and found a corner to pray by herself. She was sincere; she was pleading her case to Yahweh with all her heart. She was emotional and she was upset. In fact, she got so carried away that her words sounded like she was speaking a foreign language. Eli the priest was sitting at his post in the temple and overheard Hannah babbling.

He came over to her as tears flowed down her face in bitterness and pain as if all were lost. She was so desperate that she cried out to Yahweh that if He gave her a son, she would give that son back to Him all the days of his life and that no razor would come upon his head.

Finally Eli interrupted her. He had never seen anyone so lost and full of passion in prayer. Eli himself was given to gluttony and he and his sons had been using the priesthood to gain riches and his sons used women for their own purposes. Eli could hardly get around he was so heavy.

Eli said to Hannah, "How much wine have you had to drink? You have no business coming into the temple and speaking like a drunken woman with words that make no sense."

Hannah pleaded through her tears, but with an authority in her voice, "I have not had a drop to drink, my priest. I have a sorrow in my heart that runs to the deepest places in my soul. I have come here in faith believing that Yahweh will hear my petition."

Eli suddenly realized the sincerity of this poor woman. Words came up out of him that surprised even him, "Go in peace, and the God of Israel will grant you your petition."

Hannah jumped up, wiped off her tears. For the first time in years a joy filled her heart and a glow came to her face. She returned to Elkanah and immediately he saw a beauty that even surpassed the beauty that he always thought was in Hannah.

Elkanah said, "What happened to you?" In joy, Hannah just said she "had a great time of prayer at the temple, and is there anything she could do for him?"

The next day they returned home and songs were on the lips of Hannah all the way. Elkanah was happy and Peninnah watched closely wondering what to make of it.

Two months later Hannah missed her monthly cycle and the Word of the Lord spoken through the mouth of the priest came true. She was with child and that child was a boy. They named him Samuel which means "asked of God."

The next year at Passover Elkanah was getting ready to take the family back up to Shiloh and Hannah wouldn't go. He said, "Come, after all

God answered your prayer and we need to go and make sacrifices of thanksgiving to Him."

Hannah refused saying, "It is not time yet. I will not go up with the child until after he is weaned."

A few years later Hannah said to Elkanah, "It is now the time to take our son to the House of the Lord. I promised God that if He blessed my womb that I would return the child to him all the days of his life. So let's take three bullocks, flour, and wine to the priest and let's take our son to live with Eli so that Samuel may grow up in the House of the Lord."

When they showed up at the temple they presented themselves to Eli. He had gained fifty more pounds in the last five years but Hannah chose to fulfill her promise to Yahweh no matter how incapable Eli appeared to be as a priest.

Hannah spoke to Eli and said "do you remember me? I am the woman who five years ago came here to the temple to pray and you told me that God would answer my prayers. Well He did, and this young man here is that answer. As I promised God, I have brought him here to you to live with you and serve you in the ministry. We will supply all his financial needs while he grows here with you and learns the ways of the Lord."

Eli was speechless but he knew better than to argue. After all she said the key words: they will pay for every need, so this will be another steady source of food and money. Eli agreed and took the boy and gave him a room to sleep in.

Amazingly, over the next several years, Hannah was blessed with a total of six more children. Did Yahweh withhold the first so long just so she would give him back to Yahweh? These are surely among the mysteries of life with Yahweh.

Eli and his own two sons had lost all faith. They went through the motions of piety but Eli lived for eating the daily sacrifices that came to the Lord and his sons were given over to the flesh for any woman they could get their hands on. They even had a place in the temple where they took women, claiming that it was a proper sacrifice to Yahweh if they gave themselves to the two sons.

Eli complained to his sons about their actions but they ignored him. After all why should they believe this glutton? Besides, they did not even believe Yahweh to be real.

The child Samuel grew and everybody liked him. Eli did protect Samuel from the influence of his two sons although Samuel already knew that they were without faith. Samuel prayed and with a sincere heart observed the ways of God. He already understood that not only did Yahweh have his laws, but He also had his ways of doing things. At even such a young age there was a knowledge that Yahweh was great and greatly to be praised.

 One night Samuel was awakened by a voice calling his name. He assumed it was Eli, so he got up, ran downstairs to Eli's bedroom and called to him, "Here I am."

Eli awoke and said, "I did not call you go back to bed." A second time Samuel ran downstairs and said to Eli, "Here I am."

A second time Eli said, 'Go back to bed I did not call you."

The third time it happened it dawned on Eli that it had been the Lord calling Samuel. So he said to Samuel, "if the Lord calls you again, just call out and say 'speak Lord for thy servant hears.'"

The Lord called Samuel again, "Samuel, Samuel."

The child cried out, "Speak, for thy servant hears you."

Then the Lord spoke, a voice seemingly out of the air, as if "Someone" were present yet no one to see.

The voice gave clear words of judgment against Eli and his sons. Their sins were recognized by God and death would come one day to the two sons because Eli did not try to restrain them. In addition, the succeeding family will have no place in ministry.

The next day Eli asked Samuel "Did the Lord call again?"

Samuel said, "Yes He did."

After a pause, Eli asked, "What did He say to you?"

Samuel proceeded to tell Eli every detail of judgment that God said was coming to the house of Eli. Eli took this all in and a wave fell over him from the top of his head to the soles of his feet. It was a wave of sadness and helplessness. He had known all along that he was guilty, even though he kept saying to himself that one day he would stop all of this, he knew it was too late.

He left Samuel with words of encouragement. He told Samuel that he was a fine young man. That Samuel had shown that he worshipped the Lord with all his heart and that this was pleasing in the eyes of the Lord. Eli told Samuel that the Lord has chosen him and proved it by speaking directly to him in a way that Samuel understood. This was a special gift and calling and he pleaded with Samuel never to turn away from the ways of the Lord, as Eli had done.

Within one year both sons died in one day and at the news of their deaths Eli's heart gave out and he fell over and died.

 So as a teenager Samuel stepped into the office of the prophet for all of Israel. He grew into manhood reading God's word as written by Moses and Job before him. He studied those words and followed those directions given meticulously and sincerely.

Samuel grew into relationship with Yahweh to a level that few ever have. They had a speaking relationship whereby when one spoke the other listened and spoke back. It became apparent to all that met Samuel that if any tribe wanted to know what God would do in any situation, Samuel could ascertain what God would do every time.

Samuel was very careful with this gift of relationship. He never used his position to extract gifts or personal offerings from the people. He learned his lesson watching the ugly demise of the house of Eli. Samuel spent time daily with Yahweh. He memorized chapter after chapter of the words written by Moses some five hundred years earlier.

While Abraham was the father of the children of Israel, it was Moses who put the words down on papyrus for succeeding generations to follow. Even though they were careful in repeating the stories passed down from generation to generation, it was a good thing for words to be put down for all to read so they could not be changed or embellished to suit someone's needs.

18 David Chosen by God

CHAPTER THREE

A t age twelve, David was still a shepherd, and at this time he was camped a two day journey from the village of Bethlehem which was home. Each of the six families took turns bringing a six or seven day supply of food out to the shepherd boys from the little village of Bethlehem.

All the other family members were farming their lands for olives, grapes, and wheat. All the work was done by hand and all tribal families worked as if it were one communal farm for the tribe.

It was not a prosperous life. But they had good fields and crops and animal herds were growing. There had been talk among the tribal elders about joining forces and unifying the overall government. The issue arose because they had enemies that were attacking one tribe at a time. Thus, each tribe alone was vulnerable and they felt their unification would be in their mutual best interests.

The Philistines were their neighbors and they were a lazy lot. They invaded whenever it was harvest time because their king wanted more for his extended family than his people provided for him. They had stores of gold and silver but did not want to trade. They only wanted to steal.

The tactical problem was that no one tribe could defeat the Philistines, or for that matter, the Hittites or the Amorites who also invaded to steal. The Hittites and Amorites lived six and seven days journey away so they attacked only in the spring and fall when the bounty was greater.

The prophet Samuel travelled very light. He walked with his ever present staff and only a bag over his shoulder. He often went alone on these journeys depending on the hospitality of the people. For the people it was of the highest honor to feed the prophet.

As the prophet Samuel toured the tribes he was constantly asked for words of direction from Yahweh. Were they going to be invaded? How should they fight? Would God give them victory? At the direction of Samuel sacrificial lambs were offered to Yahweh and Samuel would intercede on behalf of each tribe for protection.

So for many years the tribes seemed protected, yet at the same time, there were constant skirmishes. While the tribes seemed able to drive the enemies back if they did invade, it always cost them a loss of part of the harvest, some lives, and they lived with a constant threat hanging over their heads.

The young men in every tribe spent time practicing with their slings. Each tribe had only a handful of swords that had been captured from invaders. One summer, as David went out to the flocks, he convinced his father to let him take the small sword with him while leading the sheep. It was about three feet long and David wanted to practice daily with it to learn how to use it effectively. He was a warrior in the making, as proven by killing the bear as a ten year old.

The men of Israel also learned to fight with goads and bows and arrows. Goads were six foot poles that they used to goad the sheep into their folds. They learned to put sharp points on goads to make them more dangerous. Not many were proficient with the bows and arrows, but they were a part of the arsenal.

Curiously, David was becoming as proficient with the chordophone as he was with the sling. He was a poet as well, and his poetry was not learned – he was born that way. The only schools at the time were those run by Samuel. They were schools of the prophet and centered on memorizing the Pentateuch, the five books written by Moses.

Each student was expected to memorize these books by the age of five. If they didn't they were dismissed from the school. School then was not for everyone. David had never been to the school, his family needed him and that was that. But he did learn to read and they had a family copy of the scriptures. So David would take pages of parchment with him to read.

One night after the sheep had been gathered into a protected area on the side of the hill; David took his chordophone and began to play. His fellow shepherds did not mind at all; in fact it seemed to quiet the sheep and helped the shepherds to sleep better as well.

> *O Lord, our Lord, how majestic is your name in all the earth!*
> *You have set your glory above the heavens*
> *From the lips of children and infants you have ordained praise*
> *because of your enemies, to silence the foe and the avenger.*

> *When I consider your heavens, the work of your fingers, the*
> *moon and the stars, which you have set in place,*
> *What is man that you are mindful of him, the son of man that*
> *you care for him?*
> *You made him a little lower than the heavenly beings*
> *and crowned him with glory and honor.*
> *You made him ruler over the works of your hands;*

You put everything under his feet:
all flocks and herds, and the beasts of the field,
the birds of the air, and the fish of the sea,
all that swim the paths of the seas.
O Lord, our Lord, how majestic is your name in all the earth!

David's singing poetry revealed his views of Yahweh. He sang of the creation and how wonderful it is. He sang of the love and power that he felt came from Yahweh. This showed an incredible perspective of Yahweh by one who was just entering puberty.

To David it would seem his heart would overflow with love for Yahweh. He was not "afraid" of Yahweh in the sense that he thought he would be punished for every wrong doing. But he had a sense of deep respect and a desire to please the Living God. He desired to live right and do right in the eyes of Yahweh.

Abishai often sat with him and listened; frequently tears came to his eyes at David's singing. Abishai leaned over and said, "I never think about the 'Lord over all the earth' until you sing about it. How do you think about such things?"

David replied, "As I look out over the hills and into the sky, I often try to count the stars. I pick out just a small square in the heavens and count. When I get to one hundred I realize that what I have counted only means that there must be ten thousand times more stars. Then I start thinking of how big they must be to be so far away and yet their light shines upon the earth.

Then I start wondering how Yahweh put them there. Then I begin to realize how wonderful and powerful must Yahweh be."

David continued, "Do you remember the last Passover Feast when Samuel came?"

Abishai said, "I'll never forget it. When Samuel offered the sacrifice of that little white lamb that had no blemish on it, the feeling I had was that I went to heaven!"

David said, "Exactly, I felt the same way. I knew then that somehow Yahweh knows us just like we know our sheep. Isn't it true that you know the name of each of your sheep as I know the name of each of mine?"

Abishai started getting excited again, "I never put that together like that. But you're right. He is our God and we are like His sheep."

David said think about this further. "When one of our sheep gets sick, we take special care of them. Remember last year when one of your sheep fell off that rock ledge that we did not realize was there and broke his leg?"

Abishai jumped in, "Yeah I remember, because I had to put that sheep over my shoulders and carry her for almost a month before she could walk again."

David said, "exactly, then imagine if we are like sheep to Yahweh would He not care for us the same way?"

Two days later it was late afternoon and each shepherd took his station as they were leading the sheep to greener pastures for the next day. David was always alert for predators at these times. It had been more than a month since they had been to this pasture.

By now David had become proficient with his sling and he was already known as the strongest and fiercest shepherd in the tribe. He could sling a stone five times farther than one could be thrown by hand, with deadly accuracy. David loved to practice with his weapons daily. Beside his sling, he swung his sword daily, not taking off heads, but tree branches.

For building his strength he lifted stones as exercise. The other shepherds thought he was not in his right mind but he paid them no attention. He was dreaming of bigger and better things than being a shepherd boy. All the tribe was talking about war and David dreamed of being the warrior to take on all comers.

As the sun was going down the shepherds began to split up to take their positions for the night.

David saw his shadow first. He was the fiercest looking lion David has ever seen. He was at the same time the most beautiful. Regally he stood there looking the part of the king of the beasts. The beast had a black mane that framed his fierce face. Suddenly, he roared a claim on the territory and attacked the sheep in all his fury.

As the lion lunged forth, he caught a lamb in his mouth. Just as suddenly the regal beast was quiet and merely trotted away to eat his prey in a quiet place.

Suddenly David jumped into the path of the lion, catching him by complete surprise. David literally took the lamb out of the mouth of the lion, and grabbed the lion by the black beard as he rose up at this threat. David then thrust his sword into the very heart of the lion. There was blood everywhere as David kept stabbing and slashing to make sure the lion was dead.

The scene was hard to believe. Here was a strapping young man (really little more than a boy), with blood from head to toe, with a bloody sword in his hand and a dead lion at his feet.

David hopped and hollered as the sheep began to scatter. The other shepherds started herding them all back together shouting out what happened? David yelled back, "It was a lion that met his match!"

David sat down, shaking and unable to contain the excitement coursing through his veins. He now felt firsthand the thrill of the warrior victory. Conquering this beast would not just be a shining moment for David; it would mark him for life.

In his young life he had dreamed already that, with God as his strength, he could do anything. But tonight the dream became a reality. David would walk differently from that night forward.

He would never be the same. His dreams were no longer fantasy. His dreams became his new reality. It was as if someone put a cloak on him and said to him - you are THE WARRIOR. He was transformed into a new person and he walked in a new form of faith. Yahweh became as real to David as his father Jesse.

The other shepherds couldn't believe it, that lion was the biggest any of them had ever seen. Lions were few and far between in this territory. They were hunted by tribal leaders because they were predators that would take down not only sheep, but any other animal, and were always a threat to the women and children. The skin for the lion would be a great prize to show to all visitors that came to the family tent.

Abishai sat there in the late hours of the night around the fire. He was almost as excited as David. He told David how he surpassed his brother Joab as the greatest warrior he had ever seen or heard about. He told

David how his brother had also killed a lion, but the lion he killed was about half the size of the one David killed.

They finally fell asleep in the third watch and slept what seemed like only minutes before it was time to get up. They had to skin the lion and Abishai promised to help.

The skin was almost too heavy to carry, so David had bundled it up and tied a vine around it so it could be dragged back home when the next food shipment came for the shepherds.

When the messenger got back to Bethlehem dragging the lion skin, everyone started asking who killed the lion and how? The messenger repeated the story that David had killed the lion by hand with only his sword and they were all amazed. They couldn't wait 'til the season ended to hear the details of the bravery of the no longer little shepherd boy. Word of David's exploits traveled far and wide. The accounts of the bear and the lion were the talk of many a gathering. At such a young age he was already gaining a reputation of fierceness and surely the warrior to come.

CHAPTER FOUR

The tribal leaders were getting impatient. They thought Samuel was truly a great man of God. They all feared him to be sure, but they also knew he was not a wartime leader. They all believed that all out war with their neighbors was inevitable. The Philistines kept sending bands of soldiers to rob the different tribes and it happened more frequently.

They felt their only solution was to find a leader on whom all the tribes could agree. They knew nothing about politics so they had no way to know how to select someone who would lead them all. They decided that, like their enemies, they should have a king.

Samuel kept telling them that God was leading them and protecting them, but they retorted if that were so, why were there more and more skirmishes all the time.

There was a division among the tribes. When their forefather, Joshua, had led the children of Israel into the Promised Land, the land had been divided into shares among each of the tribes. Those boundaries had been accepted by all of the tribes. But the two southern tribes seemed banded together and the ten northern tribes seemed banded together. The southern tribes were led by the Tribe of Judah.

The name Judah means "praise" and it was this tribe that included the House of Jesse into which David was born. All of the tribal leaders asked for a meeting with Samuel. The wisest of the leaders was named Ahithophel. In every meeting his voice made the most sense. He was close to Jesse and always asked about David. He took special interest in David as he saw something in him that transcended the ordinary.

Samuel was in the village of Ramah. He was getting up in years and he had two sons. Neither of his sons was like him at all. Samuel had made them judges in the village of Beersheba and they were both corrupt. Each went to the highest bidder so money, not justice, ruled their courts.

Representatives from each of the tribal leaders met with Samuel at Ramah. They spoke up and said, "Samuel, you are getting old and neither of your sons is like you. We want you to make us a king. We have no way of knowing how else to select one.

Samuel was hurt. He did not feel as "old" as they made him out to be. But he was faithful to the word of the Lord and interceded daily on behalf of the people. So Samuel went to pray before Yahweh to seek his solution.

God spoke to Samuel, "Hearken unto the people and give them a king! Samuel, they are not rejecting you, in reality they are rejecting me. I would be their King but they are not connecting with me on that level or understanding that possibility. Just warn them what it will be like to have a king."

Two days after departing Samuel returned Ramah and called the leaders and said, "Let me warn you what it will be like to have a king. First of all, he will demand your sons and daughters to serve him. He will take of the best of your fields, he will take a tenth of your seed for your next year's crop, and he will take a tenth of your best sheep. He will form an army that will have to be provided for, and making chariots and weapons. The day will come when you will cry at all the demands a king will make upon you and your families."

Samuel warned them further, "A king can virtually demand whatever he wants, whenever he wants it. By the way, whatever he says goes, so no more 'tribal council' unless he wants it. When he declares war, then you will have to send all of your sons to war. One other key point that will affect all of you is this: when you bring your problems to him his decision is final – there are no appeals. His word is final in all matters."

The tribal leaders were happy and they unanimously responded, "We don't care – we demand a king!"

So Samuel said, "Very well, go to your cities and villages and when I hear from God who shall be king I will let you know."

So they all returned home.

CHAPTER FIVE

There was a tribe called Benjamin. Each tribe had been named after the original twelve sons of Jacob who had been the grandson of Abraham. Benjamin was the youngest son of Jacob whose mother Rachel had died during his birth. This tribe was the smallest of all the tribes.

There was a powerful man in this small tribe named Kish. He was well known throughout all the tribes. He had a son named Saul. This son was unusual in that he was head and shoulders taller than anyone else in Israel. He was married and had children but still worked for his father as though he were a teenager.

This son Saul, as big and good looking as he was, was also insecure. He had been gangly and awkward growing up and was much teased. Other kids made fun of him, but he could not catch any of them and would not have known what to do if he had. Because of his father's strength he had found a wife, but even in that relationship his mind always went to depression and thoughts of failure.

All children among the tribes found they had a lot of lonely time to think about things. In Saul's case this had not been good. Every feast people would stare at him as if there were something wrong with him. His father would tell him they were just admiring him because he was so tall. But Saul felt they were staring at him to make fun of him.

His insecurities were not helped by how his powerful father treated him. His father did not trust him with any important jobs. He would send Saul on simple errands and he was never in charge of servants or anything of importance. He tried to do some training on how to fight.

He watched some of the other young men and he liked to throw spears. His father also bought him a sword that even as an adult he loved to play with.

One day some donkeys wandered off and Kish sent Saul and one of the servants to find the donkeys and bring them back. As they wandered off looking for the donkeys and asking neighbors if they had been seen them, they came upon the village where Samuel was staying.

Samuel was getting ready to go make a sacrifice when Saul appeared. Now the Lord had told Samuel just twenty four hours earlier, "A young man will come to you within one day and that young man is to be made the king over the people of Israel."

Samuel recognized Saul and said to him, "We will meet together tomorrow and I will tell you everything that is in your heart."

Samuel went on to say, "Don't worry about the donkeys you are looking for, they are safe and at home!" (Saul had not told Samuel he was looking for donkeys!)

Saul could barely sleep that night, it must have been around the second watch by the time he fell asleep. He was afraid and at the same time excited. He didn't want everything in his heart known by others. There were some he wanted to kill and there were some women he just wanted.

The next day Samuel began telling Saul, "You are chosen by God to be the leader of all the tribes."

Saul's first reaction was, "How can this be? I am from the smallest tribe and the smallest family in the smallest tribe so how could I be the king?"

But this was not a debate and Saul was going to have to come to grips with the word of the Lord.

Samuel told Saul, "Go to Mizpeh, a small village, and you will see things along the way that are unpredictable. If they happen it will be a sign to you that God is directing this whole adventure."

As Saul was on his way to Mizpeh he ran into a group of prophets along the road from one of Samuel's schools. They saw him and suddenly started singing and dancing and completely out of character, Saul started singing and dancing with them. He began to speak prophetic words and many people witnessed and wondered at his goings on. They knew who he was and knew he had not been a prophet, but they could not deny that he was acting like one now.

People brought gifts to Saul along the road and he was amazed. These people hardly knew him and yet they were prepared to see him and give him gifts. At every sign Saul found he was recognizing that Yahweh was up to something for sure. These people had no knowledge that Saul was to be made the king. They had just been motivated by some power beyond this world to give him gifts when they saw him. This behavior was far from normal and was to be a further confirmation to Saul that he had been chosen by Yahweh to be the king.

Samuel sent word to all the tribes to meet him at Mizpeh and he would bring them news concerning God's answer regarding a king.

When all were assembled, Saul was nowhere to be found. Samuel proceeded to read from the document he had written that set forth the rules of how society would work now that each tribe was submitting itself to a king. While he was reading this he asked the Lord where on earth Saul was and the Lord said he is hiding among the "stuff" -

meaning that he was hiding among the carts and luggage carrying the people to this meeting.

Samuel paused and whispered to two servants to go find Saul among the luggage. They found him and dragged him out, and got him to stand before Samuel. Samuel declared, "Here is the one whom God has chosen."

Many of the people cheered crying out, "God save the king!" But there were almost as many who wondered what kind of joke this was. Was Samuel picking out the least likely because he was mad at the elders? Saul was no leader and of no reputation that anyone would want to follow.

But God had touched the heart of many; they were willing to follow Saul. Some followed him back to his village of Gibeah and they were glad to serve the king. There are always those who recognize a major power shift and want to get in on the newly declared power of the land.

All the enemies of Israel heard the news. Within a month an old enemy, the Ammonites, marched on the town of Jabeshgilead to catch the new king by surprise. The men of Jabesh knew they were no match for the Ammonites, so they raised the white flag and sent a messenger to Nahash, the general of the Ammonites. The message said a curious thing: "If we do not receive any help from the other tribes within seven days we will surrender to you without a fight and we will serve you."

Well the general thought this was a bargain. He did not think in a million years any of the other tribes would be ready to come because they never had before. He thought he could take over this city without the loss of one soldier.

In the meantime the men of Jabesh sent messages to all the tribes and a messenger went to Saul at Gibeah. Saul was in the fields as usual working his father's harvest. He came in from the fields to receive the plea that was sent from the elders of Jabesh.

Suddenly, upon hearing the request, Saul was overcome with anger and an emotion the likes of which he had never experienced before. Words came out of his mouth and strength and actions burst forth in determination knowing what to do and how to do it that were indescribable. It was the Spirit of Yahweh that came over him, but he did not understand that at the time. Later Samuel explained to Saul and counseled him on how God works this way with his chosen men.

Saul took a pair of oxen that were yoked together. With his sword he cut them in pieces and sent out twelve messengers each carrying pieces of the slain oxen. He declared that one of their tribes was being attacked and he called forth for men over the age of twenty to meet him and Samuel at Bezek which was just outside the road on the way to Jabeshgilead.

Saul threatened them that if they did not come, he would do to them what he had done to the oxen. But he had not consulted with Samuel; he presumed Samuel would agree. He also showed a little insecurity by using Samuel's name as well as his own in the command to gather together all the men of the tribes.

It was quite amazing that three days after getting the message over three hundred thousand men from ten tribes and thirty thousand men from the tribe of Judah showed up for war. It was a thrilling sight. As each tribe appeared over the mountains from many directions they looked down on the plain of Bezek and saw the men arrayed by tribe, singing and joyfully ready for battle.

It was the first time for this generation to be armed and gathered as one to fight against an enemy. The momentum of the gathering carried over into the hearts and minds of every individual and leader believing that they no longer needed to be subject to the constant threats of their enemies.

Saul took charge. He gave orders to each of the tribal leaders, telling them where to line up for the attack. Obedience was the response of the day. No questions asked. Saul was on a horse while most of the rest were walking. There were less than five hundred horses available to the army but today it did not matter.

At the signal from Saul the tribes rushed upon the Ammonites and killed them at will. There was no mercy today. It was a time for killing and kill they did. At the end of the day there were not two Ammonites standing together anywhere. Victory was complete.

The tribal elders gathered around Saul with joy and thanksgiving. Samuel was present for the event, for after all, he did have a stake in the call, not only because Saul used his name, but he was the one that declared that God's choice for king was Saul.

Immediately the elders called for the dissenters to the choice of Saul for king to be brought forth and killed. They wanted to deal with the dissenters swiftly and permanently.

But Saul stepped forward and said, "There will be no executions today. It is a day of victory and celebration. It is a new day for the unification of Israel and it is time to no longer look back but for all to look forward."

Saul went on and told all the elders, "Let's go up to Gilgal and let that be the place we set up the kingdom and make sacrifices of thanksgiving to Yahweh." In great excitement they all agreed and departed early the next day.

When they got to Gilgal Samuel stood up and spoke. "Have I ever taken a bribe or a gift from any of you to sway my work for God? The leaders shouted a resounding, "NO!"

Have I miss used my office of prophet in any way for my own advantage? Again they said, "No!"

Then Samuel gave the eldership and the king a history lesson. He rehearsed for them how God, using Moses and the priest Aaron, to led the children of Israel out of the slavery of Egypt into the Promised Land that they currently inhabited. Then Samuel reminded them how, after a while, the people allowed their hearts to turn away from God and God dealt with them by allowing Sisera, a famous general of the Philistines, to overrun them and conquer them.

Samuel went on, "Our forefathers then cried out to God for mercy and God granted them mercy and sent four leaders to gather armies and to throw the Philistines out of Israel."

Samuel went on to declare for now and evermore to those who call upon Yahweh as their Lord and Savior, "If you fear the Lord and serve and obey him and do not rebel against his commands, and if both you and the king who reigns over you follow the Lord your God — then things will be good! But if you do not obey the Lord, and if you rebel against his commands, his hand will be against you, as it was against your fathers when they disobeyed his commands."

CHAPTER SIX

S aul reigned one year and then two over all of Israel. He set up two cities to base operations where he sent scouts to keep watch over enemies and to warn him of any threatening moves.

One city was Michmash in the region of Bethel and Saul stayed there with two thousand full time soldiers who were in constant training. Saul had a son named Jonathan who, although still a teenager, headed up the other base city at Gibeah with one thousand full time soldiers.

These cities were little more than villages where those who served the surrounding families lived. They began to grow during this time as soldiers away from home were requiring services. Although it was still the duty of the tribal families to send food for their sons in the army, there were common needs to take care of.

Now, at this time there was a garrison of Philistine soldiers encamped at Geba. The basic strategy of Israel had always been to fight a defensive war. They waited for the enemy to attack and they fought defensively. But there was another spirit in Jonathan. He had faith to go on the offensive.

So for the first time, Jonathan took it upon his men to go on the offensive after the enemy and fight him in his own camp. Jonathan gathered his soldiers and came at Gibeah from two angles. The Philistines were shocked as they did not even bother to have look outs because no army of Israel had ever attacked them before.

Jonathan and his army soundly defeated the Philistines. News of the defeat quickly spread among all the lands of the Philistines. They began gathering their forces to prepare for more serious battles.

At this time Saul sent out trumpeters to announce throughout Israel that "Saul has defeated the garrison of Philistines at Geba!" The announcement was made in this fashion even though Saul had not even been at Geba. Saul's insecurities were ever present. He could not even give his own son credit for taking it to the enemy. Saul was obsessed with what people might think about him.

He took credit for every success in his kingdom and blamed others for every failure when possible.

Knowing in his heart that the Philistines would mount up against them, Saul called for all the tribes to send their warriors ready for battle and meet at Gilgal.

The Philistines gathered themselves together to fight Israel, thirty thousand chariots, six thousand horsemen, and people beyond counting and they came and pitched camp at Michmash.

Michmash was on a large hill, and down into the valley and across to another hill were camped the men of Israel.

When the men of Israel saw them arrayed and ready for battle, a great distress came upon all their hearts. They started hiding in caves, in bushes, behind rocks, in pits, and along mountain sides. Some of them even left Israel and went over the Jordan River.

Oddly, the Philistines did not take advantage of the lull before the war. In reality they were just as fearful as the soldiers of Israel. They were hoping the men of Israel would all leave so they would not have to even fight.

Saul remained in Gilgal and those that stayed with him were fearful every waking moment. The Prophet Samuel had delayed in coming to Gilgal to bring the Word of the Lord, and for seven days no word about his coming came to Saul. Saul become nervous fearing everyone would leave if he didn't act quickly. So he took it upon himself to call for and offer a sacrifice to Yahweh that only the Prophet Samuel was supposed to offer.

Saul believed that as long as Yahweh put his blessings over the army and its leader, they would win, regardless of the odds. He took it upon himself to make sure Yahweh approved!

As the offering by Saul was just being finished Samuel arrived. Saul stopped everything and went out to meet him. Samuel confronted Saul and asked, "What have you done?"

Saul replied, "More people were leaving everyday and you did not come when you were supposed to. The enemy is ready for battle so I did not have a choice. I had to make the sacrifice offering to Yahweh before the Philistines waged war."

Samuel admonished him, "You have done foolishly, and you did not keep the commandment of the Lord. Therefore, instead of the Lord establishing your kingdom forever, He will take it away and give it to another. The Lord is seeking a man after his own heart."

Samuel left him and went on to Gibeah. Only six hundred men stayed with Saul and he took them and went to join Jonathan who was also at Gibeah. The Philistines remained at Michmash.

At this time in history the Philistines were the only ones in this part of the world making of swords and spears and also farming implements. They would not teach the men of Israel how to smith iron and the only way Israel could acquire such instruments was from the spoils of war.

The Philistines arrayed their troops in three companies at Michmash pointing in three different directions so that they would not have any surprises from Israel. Near the day of battle one garrison came to prepare to attack Saul at Gibeah. Saul and his six hundred men took refuge in the farthest corner of the city.

Jonathan however was not of the same temperament as his father. Jonathan was bold and strong. He was a young man of faith but at the same time he was loyal to his father and respected him.

Jonathan took his armour bearer and said, "Let's go up to these uncircumcised Philistines and see what the Lord will do. The Lord can do whatever He wants and He can save us by many soldiers or by few, it matters not with Yahweh."

The armour bearer said, "Do whatever is in your heart and know that I am with you all the way."

They climbed a rocky hill on their hands and knees. They called out to the enemy "we are coming up this way," and the Philistines responded "come up to us and we will show you a thing."

Within a matter of minutes Jonathan and his armour bearer killed about twenty men within this small field and killed their oxen as well. Suddenly a wave of fear came over the rest of the nearby Philistines. They started to shake and tremble in fear. In the confusion and in the dark of night they began beating and killing each other without any soldiers other than Jonathan and his armour bearer present.

The noise was so great that Saul asked the scouts what was going on. The reports were that only Jonathan had left the camp and all the upheaval and killing going on was being done by him. So Saul and his people gathered and came to the battle to watch as every enemy was fighting among themselves and killing one another.

The enemy turning on each other makes no sense on its own. It takes the inclusion of the influence of the supernatural to explain such events. Throughout history Yahweh has made his Presence felt in certain situations where He found agreement with someone on earth. In this case, Jonathan believed that Yahweh would intervene on behalf of the children of Israel. The faith of Jonathan was enough to motivate the influence of Yahweh upon the circumstances of war. But this faith escaped Saul's understanding and he never found it in his life.

The men of Israel then returned from every hiding ground and joined in the killing. As the Philistines fled the men of Israel chased them down. Saul knew that the victory was coming from the hand of Yahweh – there was no other explanation for defeating an enemy that was defeating itself.

Saul sent out orders during the chase to fast from all food until the enemy was completely beaten. When his men needed nourishment for battle Saul foolishly dreamed up a spiritual fast as if this would mean something to Yahweh. It did not. Yahweh was already with them and giving them victory and trying to insert some made up religious gesture was pure foolishness.

It took many days for the chasing down and killing of the enemy and the new found warriors were famished. As they were getting down to the end the soldiers started killing sheep and ox and goats and not properly cooking them but eating them while they were still bloody. This was contrary to Yahweh's dietary rules for eating.

Saul stopped going after the remaining Philistines, and he gathered all the troops so he could officially take credit for the victory and reestablish his kingdom in Israel. His insecurities continued to rule his heart.

As time went on he continued to fight every enemy that showed. He fought against the Moabites, the Ammonites, those from Edom and the king of Zobah. He continued to fight against the Philistines as well he also smote the Amalekites.

One day Samuel came to Saul and reminded him that Samuel had anointed Saul as king. He told Saul, "Now remember that the Lord wants you to destroy the Amalekites who had made things difficult for the children of Israel when they were coming out of Egypt. They had disobeyed God and now God wants to utterly and completely destroy every man, woman, child, and animal. There is to be no living thing left."

Saul went out and destroyed the enemy clearly and decisively but deliberately saved the king named Agag and kept the best of the sheep, oxen, fatlings, and lambs.

The word of the Lord came to Samuel saying, "I have changed my mind over naming Saul as king. He turns his back on me; he does not do what I tell him to do, and he makes things up as he goes along."

Samuel was sick in his heart about this. After all he had not wanted to name a king in the first place. Now that he named Saul and the Lord was going to take Saul off the throne what would happen to Samuel's credibility among the people? Samuel cried all night before the Lord.

Samuel came to Saul in the morning and Saul was excited to see him. Saul burst forth and said, "Blessed are you Samuel. I have performed the commandment of the Lord and killed the Amalekites."

Samuel said, "If that is so, then what is the bleating of the sheep that I hear and the lowing of the oxen which I also hear?"

Saul said, "Oh, the people kept back the best of the animals to sacrifice to the Lord. The rest we utterly destroyed."

Samuel said, "Saul, stay with me tonight and I will tell you what the Lord said to me before I came over here."

The next day Saul said, "Very well, tell me what the Lord said to you about me."

Samuel said, "When you were younger you were small in your own mind. Yet the Lord chose you and made you the head of the tribes of Israel and anointed you king. The Lord then sent you on a mission to utterly kill off the Amalekites. Yet you kept the spoils of war which were in this case forbidden. What you have done is evil in the eyes of the Lord."

Saul argued, "I have obeyed the voice of the Lord. I brought back king Agag and destroyed all the rest of the people. But it was the people who took the spoil of the animals because they wanted to make a sacrifice to Yahweh."

Samuel replied, "Does God prefer burnt offerings over just obeying his voice? To obey is better than sacrifice. Rebellion is just like the sin of witchcraft and stubbornness is like the tendency to sin and to worship idols. Because you have rejected the word of the Lord, He has rejected you from being king."

Suddenly it dawned on Saul what Samuel was saying and he said to Samuel, "I have sinned and disobeyed your words because I feared the people and obeyed their voice."

While the truth was coming out, it was with a whiney insecure pleading not fit for a king.

Samuel ignored his failed pleadings and said, "Bring me king Agag,"

They brought the king before Samuel and Agag said, "Surly the bitterness of death is passed?"

Samuel grabbed Saul's sword and cried out, "Agag as you have left many women childless with your sword, so shall your mother be childless today" – and he proceeded to hack Agag to death in a rage the likes of which no one present had ever seen.

All the observers had deep respect for the Prophet of Yahweh, but what they saw now was nothing less than a madman gone wild. Fear came on all the witnesses as they watched the brutality of the Prophet Samuel.

Samuel walked away with blood splattered on his garments and face and he went to Ramah without a word and without looking back. Samuel never saw Saul again the rest of his life.

Saul trudged back to his home in Gibeah to continue his rule. Although he was told the kingdom was wrenched from him, since no one else was named king Saul began to wonder if this was not just the raging of an aging Prophet.

In the meantime there was an unrelenting sadness in the heart of Samuel on behalf of Saul. Samuel had such a care for the children of Israel as they were God's people, and his heart was to care for and shepherd God's people. He often wondered if he had made a mistake anointing Saul, maybe he had somehow misunderstood God.

CHAPTER SEVEN

The Lord came to Samuel in the night and asked Samuel, "How long are you going to mourn over Saul? Pick yourself up; it is time to move forward." The Lord went on to say, "I have found the replacement for Saul, so get up out of bed Samuel and go to the house of Jesse in Bethlehem."

Samuel argued with God. "How can I go and anoint someone else? Saul is having me followed and he will come up with a reason to kill me once he learns of what I am doing."

The Lord said, "Just take a sacrificial animal with you and go to the house of Jesse to make a sacrifice if anyone asks. Now go and I will show you what to do after you get there."

Samuel arrived at the house of Jesse. The surprise and fear on Jesse's face was evident. Whenever the Prophet showed up the first reaction was fearful wondering if judgment was at hand.

Jesse welcomed Samuel and gathered all of his family together to welcome him. Samuel told Jesse to prepare the sacrifice that Samuel had brought with him. He then told Jesse to bring his sons and present them to Samuel one at a time. So Jesse started with the eldest son, Eliab, and Samuel looked him over carefully from head to toe.

The Lord spoke to the heart of Samuel and said, "Don't look at his face or how tall he is. These things don't matter. What matters is does he have a heart after me. Men always look at the outward appearance but I look at the heart."

Then Jesse presented son number two, Abinadab, and Samuel said, "Neither has the Lord selected him." Then Jesse presented Shammah, and Samuel said, "not him either."

Jesse presented seven of his sons to pass before Samuel and Samuel said the Lord has not chosen any of these.

Samuel asked Jesse, "Are there any other children?"

Jesse said, "Well I have a daughter named, Zeruiah and she has a son named Joab who is a fine young man and has shown himself strong."

Samuel said, "No, no the Lord said specifically one directly from your loins."

Jesse said, "Well yes, there is one more, but he is only about fourteen and he is off taking care of the small flock of sheep that I own."

Samuel said, "Go fetch him and we will wait." Jesse sent the next youngest son, and a day later David came running up to the home of his father.

David was out of breath, sweating with his face flushed, for he had run all the way.

He came in and started to ask his father what he wanted when he saw Samuel. David bowed suddenly for he knew he was in the presence of a man of God.

Samuel looked on David and saw his ruddy appearance and his beautiful face. He wondered in his own heart why the Lord said he did not care what the next king would look like yet here was one of the most handsome young men Samuel had ever laid eyes on.

Neither Jesse nor any of his sons knew what the purpose of this examination was all about. Finally, Samuel, as he looked on this "out of breath" David, said to all gathered, "The Lord has directed me here to this house for a special anointing that this family is to witness. This one here is called by God to become king of Israel."

Then Samuel took out his ram's horn filled with oil and held it as he began to sing and pray. Samuel prayed for over an hour. All the family of Jesse had gathered around and all began to pray and sing. David likewise joined in the singing and actually sang a few of his poems that the family had not heard before.

The atmosphere was heavenly in nature. None of the participants had ever so shut out the awareness of where they were or of the things around them. There was an overwhelming sense of the "Presence of Yahweh" in their midst. There was no personal thinking or evaluations going on. All there were ready to hear from Yahweh and do whatever He said.

At the direction of Samuel, David got on his knees and Samuel leaned over and poured oil from the horn over David's head. The oil poured down over his head and shoulders and back and face and down to his feet. As Samuel prayed and cried out to Yahweh the Holy Spirit came and filled the heart and mind of David. Samuel then proclaimed, "David will be king over Israel!" The whole family literally fell over from where they stood in amazement.

Jesse and his wife wept uncontrollably with wonderment in their hearts and minds over the ramifications of this event. Minutes turned to hours as they were now lying prostrate in awe and reverence at what seemed like the Presence of the Lord to all the gathering.

David later was told by Samuel how the Spirit of God had come over him and that from that day forward David would have a new connection with Yahweh. This connection would enable David to hear from God directly. The Spirit of God came on David to gift him with wisdom and knowledge and understanding beyond his years. He was now equipped to sense God's guidance in his life. Even though a boy chronologically, he grew with a heavenly perspective about life and the choices he would make in the coming years.

It was thrilling and power infusing.

It was hard for David to understand what was happening to him. His mind could only grasp so much. For the first time he began to understand that there was a difference between the rational thoughts in his mind and those in his heart.

David knew his heart was touched and empowered with this "infilling with the Holy Spirit of God." From that day forward he had "two sets of eyes." One pair seemed to look and evaluate what he could see naturally around him. With the other pair he could see what could happen with Yahweh's involvement.

It took a lifetime to fully realize all that this would mean to him. At this moment however, he was filled with joy and he jumped up and danced in circles crying out to God proclaiming how wonderful God is.

After all the dreams David had cultivated, he now added a newfound potential. This infusion of Power from Yahweh was tangible to David. He now believed that anything was possible. He was already feeling bolder about life and his own potential, but now he felt like he had just tapped into heaven. David believed his life now transcended what was going on around him

Samuel took David off to the side to talk with him. Samuel said, "David, the time of fulfillment to what Yahweh has done here today is in His hands. You have been introduced to the 'will of God' today. His will is realized in our lives as we obey him and follow what He wants us to do for him in this life. You are to have no higher purpose in life but to accomplish his will!"

David's whole family was overwhelmed by the moment, but in reverence, no one else said a word. There was no direction given as to how this would all take place. Was this "boy" ready to be king? No one in the family thought so. Yet they feared what the prophet said, because Samuel spoke as God, so all kept quiet and asked no questions.

*   *   *

At the same time far away in Gibeah the Spirit of God departed from Saul. Immediately, an evil spirit came upon him and troubled him. Saul suffered tormented feelings that all was lost. A deep depression came over him so he went to bed and nothing could console him.

The servants of Saul were loyal. After all, there were many benefits living in the king's household. They gathered in meetings discussing what they could do to help the king in these depressing moments. One of the servants said, "I know what he needs. When he gets like this he needs someone gifted with a chordophone who can sing sweet songs of the Lord."

Another servant jumped up and said, "I know just who to get. He is a young shepherd boy named David. I was walking the hills of Bethlehem one day and I heard this sweet melody coming over the hills and found out this shepherd boy had the gift of song and music."

The servant went on to say some things about David that surly had a prophetic sense about them. He said, "This young man not only plays beautiful music, but he is a valiant man, a man of war, and prudent in matters and handsome!"

This was quite a testimony for a lowly shepherd boy. Saul sent messengers to Jesse and he asked for David to come to him. Saul said in his message, "David has found favor in my sight so please let him come to me and I will take care of him."

Jesse received the request in amazement. No sooner had his own son been prophesied to become king and the king requests his son's presence. Yahweh surely works in mysterious ways.

Jesse sent David with food and garments, on a donkey with his chordophone to the house of the king. Whenever Saul felt depressed he called for the young David to play and sing him out of his depression. There was no personal relationship between the two. Saul would go into his fit of depression, and the servants would usher in David who played off in the corner. Saul would come out of his fit and run and hide himself in shame into his chamber. He would never speak to David.

These cycles of depression happened with regularity. In the meantime, David met Jonathan and the two became fast friends. Although Jonathan was a few years older they had much to share in faith of Yahweh. They shared a similar belief that, with Yahweh, all things were possible.

Life went on in Israel as though nothing had changed. Saul was still king. Saul did not see any evidence of a new king replacing him, so he kept on as before.

The full time soldiers kept training diligently and discussing methods of war. One soldier in particular proved very capable of leading men. He had become a great friend to Saul and his name was Abner. He was a fierce man who had little regard for life. He appeared to be loyal, but those closest to him knew he was ruthless and out for his own interests.

Abner was also a clever general who was developing the strategies for making war with the weapons they had. He also built his own following among his key soldiers. With a king that had the mood swings of Saul, he kept ever diligent to protect his own position regardless of what would happen on the throne.

During this time there was a premium on obtaining horses and swords. After every battle all the bounty was taken of chariots, horses, swords, bows and the like. The arsenals were increasing and the training of the young men was relentless. They got up at dawn every day. They ran long distances every day; they lifted stones, fought with each other to train one another, and those that had horses rode them in discipline, learning to control them in the face of battle.

The philosophy of the army was based on the belief that Yahweh was their God, but, at the same time it was well understood that for their part they needed to be prepared. They would consider themselves to be from "the army of Yahweh." So training and discipline were the order of the day.

CHAPTER EIGHT

The Philistines gathered their armies together at the town of Shochoh which was near Judah in the south of Israel. They had spied how the provisions of Judah overflowed with bounty so they selected this place to challenge Israel. They arrayed their forces near Shochoh on a mountain named Ephesdammim.

Saul gathered the men of Israel and they pitched by the valley of Elah on an opposing mountain to the Philistines. The Philistines were not by nature a brave people. Their effectiveness was best served in small bands of soldiers attacking small villages and fighting against individual families. This new strategy of facing all the tribes of Israel in battle was something of a fearful encounter.

The general of the Philistines got an idea. He had one soldier who was over nine feet tall. He came from a family of giants and had four sons who were just as tall. Goliath had armour and a helmet that made him even more imposing.

Every morning the king had Goliath stand forth and call across the valley to the army of Israel. He stood straight and tall in full armour, a helmet on his head, and chain mail on his body that was the weight of the average man of Israel! In addition, he had a spear that was bigger than most men; he had a shield, and brass plates covering his legs. He was the most formidable foe ever seen on any battlefield.

He called forth, "Choose you a man to fight me the champion of the Philistines. Let him come down to me and we will fight. Whoever wins

-- the losing man's army will surrender." He went on to say, "I defy the armies of Israel this day."

This was a clever ploy for there was not a man in Israel who would take on such a personal battle. Saul and his army arose every day in fear. Saul could only wonder what would happen if Goliath came charging over with his four sons?

Day after day the Philistines readied for battle and so did the soldiers of Israel. Every day for forty days Goliath boldly shouted his challenge.

It was merely a pantomime of war. Neither side wanted to have an all-out fight so they acted out this ruse every day to see which side would flee first.

Food was supplied to the army of Israel by the families of the tribes. While the pantomime was going on with Goliath Jesse called David who was too young to be in the army, to carry food for his brothers and others from their tribe to the battle front. David had been released by Saul from singing so he had returned to tend the sheep of Jesse.

Jesse gave David orders to carry the food and report back how his three brothers in the army were doing. David arrived early in the day when the armies had gathered together to prepare for war as they did every day with no war taking place.

David listened in fascination as Goliath challenged the army of Israel. David watched as Israel's army withdrew, frightened to death of the challenge.

David was ashamed of the fear that prevailed in the camp. He took Goliath's ranting as a challenge and insult to Yahweh. A righteous indignation rose up in his heart. While in his mind the foe was formidable to say the least, in his heart he believed that with God all things were possible.

As faith began to rise in David he walked around and asking, "What would be the reward for the man who stood up and killed this giant?"

Eliab, David's older brother got angry at David and said, "Who do you think you are asking that kind of question? You are so filled with pride and act as though you were some proven warrior. Just remember you are a little shepherd boy, so get out of here and take care of our little flock of sheep!"

Undaunted, David challenged all that would hear, "Is there not a cause to fight?" He went forward from group to group of soldiers challenging all that would listen, "How can we allow this uncircumcised man challenge the army of the Lord like this?"

The term "uncircumcised" meant that this man was not in covenant with Yahweh. He served "other" gods and had no relationship with the God of Israel.

David had a sense of national belonging to Yahweh. He believed that the twelve tribes "belonged" to Yahweh and that He was their God and they were his people. All the men of Israel were circumcised as evidence of their belonging to God.

From this viewpoint David took it as an insult that Goliath would challenge and insult the Name of the Lord. It became evident that the Holy Spirit was inspiring David to step up and take action.

Word got to Saul that a young man was going from group to group challenging them to fight. So Saul had David brought forth and asked him what he was yelling about around the camp. He took one look at David and said, "How on earth can you be here to challenge the giant?"

David said, "Your servant stands here today as a keeper of my father's sheep. One day a lion and another day a bear came to take lambs from the sheepfold. Your servant got up and killed both of them. In fact I took the lion, and grabbed the lamb out of his mouth, and then grabbed the beard of the lion and stuck him with my sword right in the heart. As I look at this giant all I see is one like a lion or bear that I have already defeated."

Saul called his servants and said to them, "Bring the king's armour to put on this young lad." As they did the armour was too large and too heavy and David could hardly move. David said, "I cannot go with this armour, I have never tested it so please let me go the way that I know."

David took his shepherd's staff and he chose five smooth stones that were lying at the bottom of the running brook close by. He put the stones in his shepherd's bag and put his sling in his hand and started to walk toward the giant.

He looked around to see if anyone else was going to join the giant. After all, when he killed him David wanted to be prepared to fight anyone with him. He had been told he had four sons, and they might come after him to seek vengeance.

Like his friend Jonathan, David walked out "in faith" believing that Yahweh would enable him victory regardless of how things looked like in the natural. David had just been "filled with the Spirit of God" and in his heart there was not a drop of fear or hesitation.

After he killed Goliath, (not *if* he killed him but *when*), he was ready for his four sons with a stone for each one in his bag. David was learning quickly that this kind of faith is a means to unleash the power of heaven into the course of things on earth.

The Philistine giant looked as David approached and began to berate him, calling him a child and saying he would feed David to the birds of the air. He began shouting to the army, "is this the best you have?" He roared in laughter and cursed David by the gods of the Philistines.

David walked closer. Anger rose up within him. He felt beside himself. He had only felt this rage and indignation before when he had challenged that lion. He sensed that at this moment he was being filled with a power and confidence born out of his own faith by the "Spirit of Yahweh."

He shouted at the giant, "You come against me with a sword and a spear, but I face you in the Name of the Lord of Hosts, the God of the armies of Israel that you have defied. Today the Lord will deliver you into my hand. Furthermore, I am going to take your head and leave your carcass and the carcasses' of your army to the beasts of the field and the fowls of the air.

"The entire world will know this day that the God of Israel is Lord of all the earth. And all will know that God does not save his children with sword and spear, because the battle is the Lord's and He will give you into my hand."

Goliath quit talking and lumbered toward David with a mocking smile on his face. David put his hand in the bag and took out one of the smooth stones, about three fingers in diameter, and began to run to meet the Philistine. David yelled out, "I come to you in the name of the Lord of Hosts, the God of the armies of Israel, whom you have defied."

David slung the stone so swiftly that no witness saw it fly. Neither did Goliath for that matter. There was one opening on the entire body of the giant. He had armour on his legs, his loins, his torso, and a helmet on his head. The only vulnerable spot was his forehead. The slung stone found its mark and sank its width into his brain and the giant toppled over as if a building collapsed in an earthquake.

David ran the rest of the way and stood over the fallen giant. He took the sword of the giant, raised it high overhead and shouted victory in the Name of the Lord. From the Israeli side David heard cheers and excitement, orders being yelled and swords being drawn. From the other side he heard cries of fear and the sound of retreat.

David raised the sword and chopped off Goliath's head. He then grabbed the head by the hair and walked off with the giant's head in one hand and the giant's sword in the other. The Philistines ran in terror and Saul's army jumped up and ran after them and slew everyone that they reached.

Interestingly, David never said a word to anyone. He took the head of Goliath and marched alone to Jerusalem. On this march in victory his heart was filled with a new strength and confidence in the Lord. He prayed and worshipped Yahweh. In his heart he loved God with all he had. He gained a new confidence in God.

He had a growing sense that his life was meant to serve the Lord and worship him all the days of his life.

When he reached Jerusalem he put the giant's head on display on a mountain that was later called Golgotha.

Also of note, his three oldest brothers who witnessed this epic battle, had a sudden change of heart and saw their "little shepherd boy brother" in a whole new light. No longer was he the dreamer claiming great exploits, they saw with their own eyes that he had become a warrior of warriors.

Saul wanted to know who David was and what family was he from so he sent Abner to get him and Saul questioned him. Saul never connected that this was the same "boy" who was the one who sang poems to relieve his depression. Saul demanded that David come to live with him again.

In the days that followed David was kept in the home of the king, he and Jonathan renewed their friendship. Jonathan was so proud of David and how he conquered the giant. He recognized the "Spirit" of God on David which none of David's brothers had understood.

They hunted together, they trained together, and they sat up late at night worshipping together as they looked over the hills and the stars of the heavens. They compared dreams and both could understand the plans of God for a people that He would call by his name.

Since the fall of Mankind God had been looking for a Nation, an identifiable group of people who would recognize Yahweh as the one true God and who would be seen as such by the rest of the world. He had begun building that identification in Abraham. And now He wanted the Nation of Israel to be known as the People of God.

David and Jonathan thought this connection between God and the people of Israel were to become more apparent to the world. They understood there was a destiny that was first promised in the Garden of Eden and clearly promised to their father in the faith Abraham.

They dreamed that the Promises of God would come true. They had both read to each other the laws for living as defined by Moses. They read scripture and believed that God was involved directly with the life of Israel. They believed that God would give them victory over their enemies every time.

In their discussions and prayer times together, they were agreed that God had promised the land to Israel and that it belonged to them and they were to conquer all threats to this land.

Even though the role of king was new to Israel, it was understood that the son of a king would succeed the king at his passing. But Jonathan knew, just as David's fellow shepherds knew, that God had a "call" on David and that he was the one who should succeed his father Saul.

One day, after worshipping Yahweh together, the two young men were alone at sunset. In the shadows falling around them a holy hush came on them both. Jonathan stood in front of David and took off his robe, his garments, even his sword and his bow and his girdle which held his weapons of war. It was a sacred moment. They both knew that God was leading this event.

Jonathan was being inspired, meaning the "Spirit of God" seemingly breathed into him, the urge to take this time to submit himself willingly to the authority of his dear friend David. He was relinquishing his right to succeed his father. He was humbling himself in recognition that the call to be king was on David.

With tears in his eyes, David was humbled and at the same time he knew it was true. So he choked out his acceptance of Jonathan's declaration and promised Jonathan that, should the day come for David to be made king, he would preserve the life of Jonathan and any of his living family. This promise was vital as the usual practice was to kill any succeeding family members of the king.

The next day, knowing nothing of the ritual that took place between Jonathan and David, Saul sent David to represent him and put him in charge of men of war. David was accepted in the sight of all people wherever he went. Even Saul's servants honored and loved David.

As David returned from battle, having defeated the Philistines, the women started singing songs about the exploits of David. He had captured the hearts and minds of the people. One of the most popular songs was, "Saul had slain his thousands, but David his ten thousands."

After hearing this song, over and over, Saul eyed David from that day forward. Saul's insecurities would flood to the surface whenever he considered the admiration the people had for David. Jealousy and envy became powerful forces in the life of Saul competing with his fits of depression for control.

CHAPTER NINE

O ne day Saul, in a fit of depression, walked by a javelin as David played his chordophone. He suddenly picked up the javelin and threw it at David. David was alert and avoided the first throw and the second one as well.

Saul was afraid of David. He was conflicted and knew he could not simply get rid of David. So the idea came to him to make David a captain over 1,000 soldiers and send them to wage battles with the Philistines secretly hoping he would die in battle.

Every time David was put in harm's way he found victory. Saul would send him to wage war against a foe superior in numbers but it never mattered to David. He would go forth in the name of the Lord with his trained superior forces and defeat every enemy he faced.

An idea came to Saul. He was willing to give one of his daughters to David in marriage so he picked out his daughter Michal. He knew that Michal was strong-willed and David would have his hands full with her. He made the offer to David through his servants.

They told David that he found favor with Saul, that Saul wanted to make David a son-in-law. David was very humbled and replied, "How can I, such a poor man, become the son-in-law of the king?"

Saul had prepared his servants to say that a dowry, due to the king for his daughter, was not necessary. The agreement would be if David would bring the foreskins of one hundred Philistines that that would be dowry enough. Saul of course was thinking that there was no way David could do this, and in fact might die trying.

David took some of his men and took the foreskins of two hundred of the Philistines, instead of one hundred, tied them together in a string and presented them to Saul. Instead of seeing the challenge kill David, Saul had to witness the increase of the reputation of his number one warrior.

So David took Michal as his wife which only made Saul yet more afraid of David. Moreover, Michal loved David and Saul, knowing how cunning his daughter was, could only view David as a greater threat.

David was careful how he walked and how he talked. He honored others and he was humble before all. But on another level there was much confusion in David's mind. After all, the Prophet of God, Samuel, had "anointed" him to be the KING of Israel! Yet, there already was a king with no end in sight.

In fact, the current king hated David and was out to kill him. So what on earth was Yahweh doing? Even more importantly what was he going to do? He had no idea who he could trust other than Jonathan. But Jonathan still had to respect his father and it would be unfair for David to drive a wedge in that relationship. Everyone seemed to want the favor of the king over the favor of "the poor shepherd boy who became a warrior." His reputation for slaying his "tens of thousands" did not matter very much if the king wanted him dead.

This ongoing stress seemed to attack the heart of David. He would not allow his mind to consider thoughts of killing the king. He loved God. He worshipped God, and it was only in his times of worship that he could find a rest in his heart that everything would work out in God's timing.

David had to rely on the fact that his kingship would come in due time, for he had been assured it was God's will and he believed it.

David gave his heart expression to glorify God at all times. He came to realize, that although he had to be alert at all times and aware of the threats against him, he trusted God with his life. In his heart he believed it was God's responsibility to bring together the confluence of events required that his day to be king would come about.

Saul heard the news of another threat by the enemy was coming so he sent David to battle. David and his personally trained warriors dispatched the Philistines quickly and David returned a victorious general to the delight of the people and their songs of adoration.

Saul called his trusted general Abner and said, "Go visit David's home tonight and kill him! He cannot be trusted as he gathers all the glory to himself."

One of the servants overheard the order and ran to Michal to tell her of the plot, "Your father has just issued an order to Abner to kill your husband David."

Michal ran to her husband to tell him the news. She begged him to run while she prepared a ruse.

They kissed in desperation with the threat at hand, and David sneaked out the back window in the dark and fled alone.

Michal went to their bedroom and laid a statue in their bed, and some straw to look like a head.

There was no way David could take Michal with him as he fled empty handed. She would be safe after all she was the king's daughter.

The aides to Abner came in the middle of the night. Abner was careful so there would be no witnesses to the murder of David.

They came into the bedroom and discovered the ploy. They ran to Saul and he sent out a band of soldiers to hunt and kill David. Meanwhile David was on the run, he had no provisions, no weapons, no friends to turn to, and so he just ran.

While on the run with tears streaming down his cheeks a song rose out of his heart, Psalm 59:

Deliver me from my enemy, O God: defend me from them that rise up against me. Deliver me from the workers of iniquity, and save me from the bloody men. For, lo, they lie in wait for my soul: the mighty are gathered against me; not for my transgressions, nor for my sin, O LORD...

He can think of only one place to go - to the man of God, Samuel. When he quickly travelled all night and finally arrived at Ramah. He was out of breath, hungry and desperate. He found Saul and said, "The king has issued a call to kill me, what should I do? I need answers; after all, you anointed me king!"

Samuel paused, not quite sure what to do either. He grabbed David and pulled him inside. "Saul has spies watching my every move. You cannot be seen here for he would like nothing better than to kill us both."

But Samuel was too late, David's arrival had already been seen and a runner was at that same moment on the way to report to the king.

Samuel told David, "We can't stay here; Saul will know shortly that you came to me. Let's go to the village of Naioth where I will hold some meetings with some of my students."

Samuel was holding "prophetic meetings" with his students at Naioth. In these meetings all present would begin singing and many playing chordophones and trumpets. Songs of joy and deliverance could be heard and the "spirit of prophecy" would come on the students and those present. They felt their songs and words were from Yahweh.

Saul met with Abner and said, "We missed our chance. Since he ran I can't just send out the troops to kill him. The people could very easily rise up against me, as they love him so much. Send messengers to David to try and persuade him to come back."

When the messengers came to get David, the "spirit of prophecy" came on them as they came into the presence of the worshippers.

This went on for days, and Saul sent more messengers when the first ones did not return. Then the third time Saul sent messengers and again they did not return. So Saul determined to go himself. When he got to Ramah he got directions to go to Naioth. As he set out to go there the "Spirit of God" came upon Saul. He walked and prophesied or spoke words from God and worshipped God with all his heart.

When he came to Naioth, he came before Samuel and continued to prophesy. A strange sensation came over Saul. He continued praying and prophesying and took off his clothes. He stripped completely naked and lay down in the presence of Samuel - naked for a full night and a full day. It was almost as if he were in a drunken state. Saul lost track of time and was just caught up in the euphoria that transcended the limitations of human reasoning.

In the meantime, David fled and went back to Jonathan. They met in secret and David with tears in his eyes begged, "Help me my brother Jonathan! How can my loyalty be questioned? You must find out if your father will really kill me or is this just one of his mood swings?"

Jonathan did not know the answer but agreed to help. They agreed on a signal system for Jonathan to find out and warn David.

The conflict David faced was beyond rational understanding. As he hid in the forest his mind struggled to grasp his situation. "On one hand I was anointed to become king of Israel. On the other hand the present king is out to destroy me. "My heart is motivated to fulfill the 'will of God.' But how can I take it upon myself to kill the king?

"I believe that Yahweh has installed Saul as king and it cannot be for me to dethrone him. But, I cannot "see" the solution to this dilemma. My heart tells me to stay on the run."

Saul finally returned to the palace. He and Jonathan had much discussion during which at first, he denied he wanted David dead, he finally admitted he would kill David. Jonathan then revealed to his father his covenant with David which nearly caused Saul to lose his mind. Jonathan then had the boldness to intercede with his father on behalf of David but it was to no avail.

In fact, Saul thought his son was naïve to be so accommodating to his "friend David." Didn't he know that when David became king he would, out of necessity have to kill Jonathan. Yes, even though Saul knew nothing about the anointing by Samuel over David, he knew in his heart that David would be the next king.

There was nothing Jonathan could say or do. There was no way to explain the mutual love that David and he had. Their love bond was even closer than the love of a man for a woman. This man's love for another man is often ridiculed and misunderstood but it had nothing to do with a physical intimacy.

A man can love another man because they have a connection of the soul. It is a connection that is filled with understanding and acceptance. It is a bond of reliability and confidence and trust between two men that only seems to happen once or at the most a few times in life.

Jonathan signaled David that his father would kill him if he caught him, so he urged him to flee. Again, David had no plan and he wondered where he could find sanctuary. He took off again not having time to gather provision or weapons.

David got an idea as he was running for his life. He went to a city called Nob. There was a priest there named Ahimelech and that was where he left Goliath's sword to be put on display.

When he got there Ahimelech quickly questioned him, "Why are you travelling alone. The general of the king's army would not travel alone unless there was trouble between them."

David lied claiming, "I am on a secret mission for the king, I left in such a hurry that I and the few soldiers that came with me are hiding in the field and we need food."

The priest said, "The only food he had was the "shewbread" or the bread that was sacrificed to Yahweh."

David said, "Very well, we will take that." Then David asked, as if he did not know, "Do you have a sword? I left in such a hurry I did not even have time to go and get my sword."

Ahimelech said, "The only sword I have belonged to the giant whom you slew." So David took the bread offered to God and the sword of the dead giant and fled as soon as possible.

Unnoticed by David or Ahimelech there was a man sitting and resting on the ground named Doeg. Doeg was the head of all the king's sheep herds. Oddly enough the name Doeg means "fear." This man was a fear speaker and his words carried fear in them. As soon as Doeg returned he reported to Saul what favor Ahimelech had shown David. Fear fell on Saul and action was required.

The question became for David, where to go to now? As he walked this idea came into his head. "What if I go to one of the enemies and seek sanctuary? I will go to the king of Gath, for he was king over the giants and Goliath, and he might love to have me on his side,"

David showed up in Gath and presented himself to the gate before king Achish. The servants ran to the king and David could overhear them tell him that David was there.

They said to the king, "This is the man that they sing about that kills his ten thousands while Saul only kills his thousands. He must be here for the wrong reasons."

David realized he made a dreadful mistake. Suddenly the idea came to him that he would play the mad man. They came back out to the gate to open it to take David into custody and suddenly David was hunched over with spittle dripping from his mouth. He started yelling, "O Achish let me in I am the great David." And he began laughing and saying things that made no sense at all.

The servants and the king looked on in amazement and the king said, "Why would I want this madman in my presence? Send him away."

So David stumbled away keeping up his ruse as long as he was within eyesight of the servants.

CHAPTER TEN

As a former shepherd boy David knew the mountains and the caves of Israel and knew how to navigate them and find his way. There were several cave systems that went on for days to explore and were filled with hard to find rooms and connections that sometimes you had to crawl through to go from one to the other.

David decided to go to the cave system at a place called Adullam. This place was probably the most complicated series of caves in all of Israel. Very few people could navigate around this territory and it was easy to hide even a small army here.

This area was arid and rocky. It was the home of White Mountain goats, with few trees, and not much water. There were some streams in some of the caves, but otherwise the area was virtually uninhabitable.

So word got out that David was hiding there. But every day David figured out how to navigate his way through and around this cave system. Again his problem was finding provisions.

Word got back to the house of Jesse that their son was hiding here. They spread the word as they believed that David could gain support and that there were many that believed the king was wrong in his treatment of David. David had been a hero warrior and brought much victory to the people of Israel. And no one knew of any legitimate reason that the king should want to kill David.

Strange phenomena took place. People all around the country started to come to the cave of Adullam. But the people that came were an unusual lot. The men that were feeling like their life was a mess and feeling great distress came to get away. Others that came were in debt and had no way to pay their bills. Still others were just discontented and wanted to change their lives.

The total of all the men that came were four hundred. Some had family with them so there were about twelve hundred people that all came to follow David. It was a bizarre gathering to say the least. But each one that came pledged allegiance to David and he became their captain.

He began training and organizing them immediately. He required a discipline that each one, although most had never done so before, agreed to follow. They set up groups of fifties and hundreds and David built a chain of command, making personnel decisions based on his own perceptions of what he saw in the men.

The first man David chose was a man named Adino. Adino was a formidable man who later distinguished himself in battle by killing an astounding 800 men in one battle in one day. Adino was in charge of the first 100 men.

The second man David chose was a man named Eleazar. Eleazar later slew so many Philistines in one day that his sword became stuck to his hand and he could not let it go for over 3 days. It was as if his sword had attached to his arm. He also was in charge of 100 men.

The third man of note that David selected after knowing these men for only a few days was a man name Shammah. Shammah had distinguished himself already when a contingent of fifty Philistines came to his small farm of forty acres. For the second year in a row they came at harvest time to steal his harvest. This time however, he stood in the midst of the field and said, "Enough is enough. These are my lentils,

I planted them and I will harvest them," and he proceeded to kill the entire contingent in one day with his sheep's goad as his only weapon.

A fourth man was revealed during this time and that was David's cousin Joab. His cousin was older than David was and he was a strong man and clever. David learned to rely upon him as Joab seemed to always know his place and that place was under the authority of David.

At this time David took his mother and father to the king of Moab and asked for sanctuary for them until he could find out what the Lord would do for David. The king of Moab was a distant relative and David promised to send provisions from the spoils of war.

There was an accepted prophet in the group from one of the schools of Samuel. His name was Gad. He came to David one day and said it is time to leave this cave and go back to your families' rightful home land in Judah.

David was quick to obey when he felt convinced that it was Yahweh speaking to him. So he took his small army and went to the forest at Hareth.

Saul heard news that David was now leading a group of men. No one knew the exact size but it was more than a few. Saul spoke out to his servants that were gathered around him, "Why does no one care what happens to me? My own son makes a league with this rebel, and no one tells me. Do I not have anyone with me that will keep me informed of these things?

Doeg stood up and said, "My king, I saw the priest Ahimelech give David bread and a sword."

Saul sent for the priest and his extended family and all of the priests that were under Ahimelech. When the priest and his family arrived the king questioned him, "Did you conspire with David, the son of Jesse when he came to your temple and did you give him food and a sword?"

Ahimelech, with a sense of fear in his heart, spoke up in defense quickly and clearly, "Who is more loyal to my king than David. He is your son in law, he goes at your bidding, and he is faithful in his service to you."

Ahimelech went on, "Let me be clear, I did not seek a word from Yahweh on behalf of David. I did not give him any guidance or direction. I had no idea of the trouble there was between the two of you."

Saul went into a rage, "Kill him and kill all of his family," he shouted at the top of his lungs. No one jumped forward to carry out the order. After all this was a man of God and most of those around Saul were unsure of his vengeance toward David as it was. Finally his chief shepherd, Doeg, came forth to carry out his command. Doeg executed some eighty five priests under the leadership of Ahimelech on the spot.

Then Saul sent his men to Nob and continued the slaughter and there he killed every man, woman, and child and every animal that resided in that village. It was a dark day for the land of Israel. The darkness in the heart of the king could no longer be contained or explained away.

But also another dynamic arose out of the massacre. Every city and village was now greatly afraid to come to the aid of David. Yes, he was a hero, but in many eyes he was now the fallen hero. If the king would destroy an entire family and village and of all things a conclave of holy men, who inadvertently gave aid to David, no elders in all of Israel were going to interfere with the king's clear desire to kill or banish David and his followers from the land of Israel.

One priest had escaped the massacre and his name was Abiathar, a son of Ahimelech. He found David and told him all that transpired. David encouraged him by telling him that his enemy is also David's enemy. So he stayed with David and that day began an important relationship between the man of God and David that would last a lifetime.

This was a tragic time and showed the power of the evil force driving Saul within his soul. It made David very upset that the priest he had lied too paid with his life for just offering some help to him. David drifted off by himself that night and got out his chordophone and wrote this song about Saul recorded in Psalm 52:

Why do you boast of evil, you mighty man? Why do you boast all day long, you who are a disgrace in the eyes of God?

Your tongue plots destruction; it is like a sharpened razor, you who practice deceit. You love evil rather than good, falsehood rather than speaking the truth.   **Selah**

You love every harmful word, O you deceitful tongue! Surely God will bring you down to everlasting ruin:

 He will snatch you up and tear you from your tent; he will uproot you from the land of the living.   **Selah**

The righteous will see and fear; they will laugh at him, saying, "Here now is the man who did not make God his stronghold but trusted in his great wealth and grew strong by destroying others!"

But I am like an olive tree flourishing in the house of God; I trust in God's unfailing love forever and ever. I will praise you forever for what you have done; in your name I will hope, for your name is good. I will praise you in the presence of your saints.

David was a man who as fear would try to come into his heart, would sit down and sing courage into his own heart. Every poem he wrote seemed to describe his pain but by the end would believe a relief was on the way. That relief was always coming his way from the Lord. He believed that, it gave him strength and enabled him to stand in the face of all adversity.

David had spies all around the country keeping him informed of the goings on in the land of Israel. Word came to him that the Philistines were getting ready to attack one of the few walled cities of Israel named Keilah. So David called Abiathar to bring with him the ephod to seek the Lord on behalf of David.

The ephod was like a container that held two objects that were used to divine the mind of God. They were the Urim and Thummim. This container was sometimes attached to a linen garment worn over the shoulder of the priest and at other times was merely set on the table in the Tabernacle of God. Abiathar was qualified to use the ephod to seek the mind of God for the decision at hand.

David enquired of Abiathar, "Shall I go and fight the Philistines?"

Through Abiathar the Lord said, "Yes go and fight the Philistines and save Keilah."

So David went to his key leaders and said "Let's go and fight the Philistines at Keilah and the Lord will go with us."

His men responded, "We are just getting started. Our disciplines are not ingrained yet and our soldiers are not ready to take on such a formidable foe at this time."

So David called Abiathar a second time and asked, "Should I go and fight the Philistines?"

The Lord told him a second time, "Yes, go down to Keilah, for I will deliver the Philistines into your hands."

This reassured David that it was the thing to do. David went to his leaders a second time, but did not ask them anything, this time he just told them that they were going based on a "word" from the Lord. They were somewhat reluctant but gathered themselves and their men and agreed to go with him. It was not that they were cowards, on the contrary over the coming years they would show bravery and thirsts for war like very few others have in history.

They went into the battle and with great success they defeated the Philistines, and they took all their cattle that were used as provisions for the Philistines, as well as they took all their weapons, and any other bounty they had with them. They celebrated in Keilah and the inhabitants were glad to celebrate with them providing food and drink.

But Saul had his spies as David had his. Saul was told what happened and where David was now. David, on the other hand, was told that Saul knew where he was and that he would come after David and his men.

David went to Abiathar again and enquired as to whether they could find sanctuary by staying in Keilah or not.

Abiathar came back and said, "The Lord said the people of Keilah would turn them into Saul, so they should flee back to the wilderness where the Lord would keep the safe."

So David and his troops, which now had grown to 600 men, took their leave of Keilah and fled to multiple hiding places throughout Judah.

David ended up in a mountain called Ziph. Saul sought David every day. Saul was becoming so obsessed with David that he often thought of nothing else. He just knew that David was going to try to take his kingdom. Here was Saul who at one time did not think he should be king; by this time he felt he deserved to be king.

The people showed their respect to him and they honored him and they gave him whatever he wanted. Who was going to let some teenager take that away from him? Besides, Samuel had lost his credibility and had proven to Saul that he could not rely on him. After all what right did he have to say that God was going to take away his kingdom? He had not taken it yet, so Saul felt like since God had not taken it, he surly was not going to let David take it either.

The men of Ziph knew David and many of his men were hiding out in their territory. So they sent emissaries to Saul to tell him that they would help Saul capture David. Saul, of course was delighted that he finally found some people that were loyal to him and not to David.

So they agreed to go throughout their land and find the exact location of David and then they would let Saul know exactly where he was. In the meanwhile, David's spies were completely informed of the plans and ran to alert David.

David seemingly trapped again, walked off and sought the Lord, (Psalm 54)

Save me, O God, by thy name, and judge me by thy strength. Hear my prayer, O God; and give ear to the words of my mouth. For strangers [the Ziphites] are risen up against me, and the oppressors seek after my soul: and they have not set God before them. Behold, God is my helper: the Lord is with them that uphold my soul. He shall reward evil unto my enemies: cut them off in thy truth. I will freely sacrifice unto thee: I will praise thy name, O LORD; for it is good. For he hath delivered me out of all trouble: and my eye hath seen the desire upon my enemies

So David, in faith, fled to another area called Maon. Saul and his men were in the chase. David and his men were on a mountain in Maon and Saul got his men together and encircled the whole mountain. The end seemed at hand. David had made a crucial mistake by not having an escape route available should a charge by Saul take place.

Just then messengers came to Saul with bad news. The messenger warned, "Come quickly the Philistines have invaded Israel and they will cause great loss if you don't act quickly."

They called the name of this place, Selahammahlekoth – which means the "cliff of escapes" for the urgency was so great for Saul to leave that he could not take time to stay and defeat David. David in amazement with the timing of the news, escaped out of the certain hand of his enemy.

The Philistines had heard of the division between Saul and David so they thought this would be an opportune time to send their forays into Israel and take advantage of the split.

On the other hand for Saul the number one concern was to preserve his kingship. He knew that the multiple threats of the Philistines and their invasion were more of an immediate threat to his kingdom than David so he would have to leave David for another day.

David took the opportunity to flee to the cave systems of Engedi. They would have more control of the environment there and could not be easily surrounded or captured. They would also be away from the eyes and ears of those who would seek the king's favor.

Saul took his key forces to attack the Philistines and his forces showed their superior training. He was able to defeat the Philistines at each encounter during these days. The Philistines still hadn't caught up to the discipline and training that the armies of Israel were experiencing.

CHAPTER ELEVEN

There were problems for David that went beyond just the fact that the king wanted to kill him – if that weren't enough. As a student of the Torah and all the writings of Moses, David was a man under authority. And as such he was to respect that authority in the person of King Saul. This respect and submission was a driving force in the life of David.

David would hold to his honor above his own needs. But just for a moment David considered an alternative. If David were to kill Saul before Saul killed him then what would happen?

He doubted that the people of Israel would want David to be the one to succeed Saul under those circumstances. If the king's blood were on his hands there would be rejection in many quarters for David trying to assume the kingship. This would jeopardize any possibility of uniting the nation under God.

It would certainly not be the kind of legacy that David was seeking. He considered himself a "man of God." As such, he wanted to live beyond reproach and wanted to have the reputation of a good and just man.

His heart would not allow entertaining such thoughts beyond a fleeting consideration. While his mind might wander to consider such thoughts they would be short lived. Even at this emerging age of leadership David's heart ruled his life. It was in his heart that he allowed God to rule his life.

He wanted to care for the people just as he had cared for his father's sheep. He wanted to establish Israel as the greatest nation on earth. He believed in the destiny of "God's people." Through them God intended to show himself as God to all people of all nations.

David believed the destiny of Israel went beyond their needs and that God intended to reveal his salvation to all the people through all of history beginning in Israel.

So with this conflict raging in his soul David led his men to the caves of Engedi. Word of course got to Saul so he took 3,000 of his full time highly trained soldiers with him to find and kill David and what Saul thought were David's few hundred ragtag followers.

So Saul and his men came to the rocks of the wild goats that lived in the region of Engedi. They had marched all day and got there in the early evening and were seeking the right place to set up a protected camp area. Camp was set up, with fires to cook the food. The troops were exhausted, and the men settled down to rest for the night with of course sentries and lookouts.

Meanwhile David had gathered one of his key lieutenants, his lifelong fellow shepherd boy, Abishai, and a couple of men and they crept into a nearby cave. Early in the dark morning when sleep was at its deepest Saul rose up to defecate. Abner waited outside so as to give Saul privacy and had no idea that anyone else was in the cave with him.

When Saul came in David's men began to whisper excitedly. They were telling him, "God has delivered your enemy into your hands!" Abishai chimed in and whispered "Let me take him now for you."

But David restrained him, "Do not destroy the king, who can put forth his hand against the Lord's anointed and be guiltless?" David took his sword and cut off a piece of the robe of Saul that he had cast aside.

David and his men then left the cave through the back way. They got to the safety of a small mountain within shouting distance.

David stood up and called out to Saul, "My lord the king."

Saul was just coming out of the cave oblivious that anything had happened. He heard the cry of David and called out, "My son, is that you?"

David bowed his whole body in reverence to the king and said, "My king, why do you listen to those that claim I seek your harm?"

David went on with an impassioned plea in his voice, "Today the Lord has delivered you into my hand in that cave you just came out of. I had many urge me to take your life right then and there. It was mine for the taking. But my heart would not agree. The words rose in my bosom that I would not put forth my hand to harm my lord for he is the Lord's anointed man.

"Look here in my hand, this cloth that I am waving is a part of your garment. That is how close I was to you and how vulnerable you were to my sword.

"This should prove to you that there is no evil in my heart against you. I have not sinned against you and yet you still hunt for me as for a dog."

With tears in his eyes and pain in his heart David went on, "The Lord judge between you and me and may the Lord avenge me of harm from you, but my hand will not rise up against you."

David then quoted a saying, "As says the proverb of the ancients, Wickedness proceeds from the wicked: but mine hand shall not be upon thee."

David's outburst continued and he repeated, "The Lord judge between you and me and may He look on and plead my cause and deliver me out of your hand."

Saul was stunned. He had 3,000 witnesses hearing the case presented by David. No one moved a muscle throughout the entire pleading. David was moved with passion and tears yet there was a power in his words that went to the heart of everyone who heard them.

Saul had to be careful now. He could order his army to charge and catch and kill David but then what. The witnesses would long remember the words of the legendary hero who could have killed the king and chose not to, but rather chose to let God decide such things.

Saul himself was touched by the passion of the moment and the sincerity of the words. In fact tears came to his eyes in a moment of clarity wondering why he was after David in the first place.

Saul called out to David in a humble fashion, "David, you are more righteous than I am, and you have rewarded me good but I have rewarded you with evil."

Saul went on quite logically, "Here I was put right into your hand to do with as you pleased yet you chose not to kill me. I pray the Lord will reward you well for withholding your hand to kill me today."

Saul paused and the next words were heard by all, and they were words that caused whispering and wondering for the rest of Saul's life, "It has been confirmed in my heart that you will be the next king of Israel. God will establish it in your hand and you will not have to take it to get it.

"I ask you to swear to me that you will not kill any of my offspring when you do."

David was stunned himself. He could hardly believe what he and all those witnesses had just heard. Saul was acknowledging that David was to be the next king!

David called out, "I swear an oath to my king that I will bring no harm to any of your family and I will preserve your name as the first king of Israel."

As Saul seemingly departed David still did not trust what he had just seen or heard. He just wasn't sure of what would happen next. Was the king merely saying these words because of the witnesses, but did he mean it? As David and his men lie in wait for Saul and his army to depart David's heart brought forth a new song,

Be merciful unto me, O God, be merciful unto me: for my soul trusts in thee: yea, in the shadow of thy wings will I make my refuge, until these calamities are over.

I will cry unto God most high; unto God that performs all things for me. He shall send from heaven, and save me from the reproach of him that would swallow me up. God shall send forth his mercy and his truth.

My soul is among lions: and I lie even among them that are set on fire, even the sons of men, whose teeth are spears and arrows, and their tongue a sharp sword.

Be thou exalted, O God, above the heavens; let thy glory be above all the earth. For they have prepared a net for my steps; my soul is bowed down: they have digged a pit before me, and in the midst whereof they are fallen themselves

All parties returned quietly to safety.

86 David Chosen by God

CHAPTER TWELVE

While there was relief in a sense, David knew it was only temporary. He knew all too well the mood swings of Saul and there was no way he thought this was all over. He knew given the chance that Saul would kill him regardless of what he said in a moment of shame.

David himself was getting lonely on the run. His wife had not been with him as she was the daughter of the king. So much time had passed that Saul, in trying to punish David any way he could, gave Michal in marriage to someone else in the king's court. It added to the pain in David's heart but he chose to go forward, regardless of what he suffered along the way.

To add to the painful times the great prophet Samuel had died. This was a loss to the nation but also to David for it was Samuel who had anointed him to be king one day, and who would believe that now. After all only his family had witnessed the event and their testimony would not carry much weight throughout the nation.

So David is single, his future more uncertain than ever, and he is still on the run. David felt he could not stay in any one place too long. He needed to provide a moving target for the superior forces of the king. All along, whenever they fought the Philistines and captured bounty, David would send an offering to the elders in Judah. He was always thinking of the future and wanted to stay in good graces with the people.

In addition, he kept his men from looting any farms or villages in their travels. The king had published the words that David was in rebellion.

But David did not want to give any proof that this was true. He wanted to maintain his image as hero and great warrior and not as a thief or as a threat to the common people of the nation.

As the nation mourned the death of Samuel there was a great gathering funeral at Ramah where Samuel was to be buried. David of course could not attend the funeral, so he went with his men down to the wilderness of Paran. This place was quite close to the Sea of Galilee and near Carmel. In this region was a very wealthy man named Nabal.

Nabal had over three thousand sheep and over one thousand goats and it was shearing season in Carmel. He was one of the richest men in all of Israel. He also had a beautiful wife who was much younger than him. The wealthy could pretty much take their choice in the days of arranged marriages in Israel. He could provide any father with a wonderful dowry and who would turn down such a thing in this time in history.

So, David sent ten of his young men down to Nabal to appeal to him for provisions. The young men came to Nabal and presented themselves.

One spoke up and said, "We are here representing David and that David was requesting any help that came to Nabal's heart to share with David and his men. We have come in peace and have already proven that David was peaceful toward your holdings."

He went on to say, "We are appealing on the basis that we have been near your herds for many weeks and have not taken any sheep and have not harmed any of the sheepherders that work for you."

Nabal was not only a wealthy man but also a cantankerous man. He was gruff with everyone and especially gruff to those who worked for him. He was a great friend to King Saul and could walk into the king's court whenever he felt like it. He was churlish and greedy and was from the house of Caleb who had been one of the great men of faith as the children of Israel came out of Egypt. Nabal was a man of influence although no one liked the man.

His answer to the ten young men was this, "Who is David and for that matter who is Jesse?" Nabal knew that Jesse did not even have one hundred sheep compared to his holdings it was nothing. Nabal went on, "Why should I give food or aid to a rebel that belongs to my workers?"

David's young men returned with the report. David became enraged and he yelled to Abishai and Joab, "Everyone get your sword let's go and deal with this rich man who thinks he is untouchable."

In the mean time one of Nabal's servants sneaked away to tell his wife Abigail how her husband had mistreated David's men and surly disaster would come their way. Abigail was not only beautiful but she was clever and wise in her beauty. The servant appealed to her that Nabal would get what was coming to him for he was the son of the devil. Pretty bold speaking for a servant, yet he somehow knew that Abigail already agreed with this accusation.

Abigail immediately took charge. She knew that David was capable of destroying everything and everyone associated with Nabal. So she had food prepared, hundreds of meaty cakes and wine, and killed and dressed five sheep and breads for David and his men. She then got on a donkey and went to meet David on his way to kill Nabal.

David was livid with only thoughts of retribution. He was just telling his troops, "I protected this man's sheep and goats and servants and this is his response to me? There is to be nothing left by dawn. I want everything and everyone destroyed. Everybody got it?"

Then this beautiful damsel shows up in front of him. She jumped off her donkey and ran over to David and fell at his feet. She humbled herself and from this kneeling position she begged, "Please forgive us for what my husband has done to you and your men?"

She received permission to speak again and she began her further appeal, "Please don't regard this man Nabal for he is certainly the son of the devil. He is foolish and in this case has done a very foolish thing to refuse to give some provision to the wonderful man David and his followers."

She went on, "Had I seen your young men I would have given whatever provisions my lord desired. I pray your enemies will suffer as Yahweh blesses my lord in all that he does. Surly my lord has had integrity and his actions have been led by the Lord all the days of his life.

"Now I pray you will forgive thine handmaid and accept the offerings that my servants bring to you and your men this day."

She then made a change in her speaking that David noticed right away. It was almost prophetic in nature and David accepted it in that light.

She went on, "Yes, there is a man that pursues you and he seeks your soul. But I pray that your life will be protected by the life in Yahweh, and that your enemies' lives would be slung out as if they were in the middle of a sling."

Abigail then got even more direct, "And when the Lord shall have done all the good that He has promised my lord, and when He shall make you ruler over Israel, then may there be no cause for grief to be remembered by shedding blood today."

Abigail finished with this, "May my lord remember me in that day of triumph?"

David felt a great touch from heaven in this woman. His anger completely left him and he said to her, "Blessed be the Lord God of Israel who sent you to me today. Blessed be your advice and I pray the Lord will bless you personally for your obedience to him to come to me and intercede.

"You may go home now in peace for we will not lift a hand against you or your household this day for I receive you and accept your appeal."

Abigail returned home and her husband was already beginning the feast of celebration for finishing the shearing of the sheep and the great gain it would bring to his household. She said nothing of what she had done and the party went on almost all night with much drinking and merriment.

The next morning she felt she had to tell Nabal what had happened. She was proud of the results for her appeal had saved Nabal and all his wealth. After Nabal sobered up she sat down with him and told him what had transpired with David.

Nabal had a heart attack on the spot. His heart became like a rock, but he held on for ten days before he died. He could not talk in that time and all the servants could do was hope he did not recover. Abigail agreed with the servants.

Word came to David and he immediately sent a few men to go to Abigail and ask her to join David. There was no mourning time needed for this widow and she gathered her five young maidens that tended to her and came to David as fast as she could get there

Abigail became his wife and loyal companion from that day forward.

CHAPTER THIRTEEN

Saul was growingly obsessed with the very existence of David. He thought about him day and night. When every battle that he fought in was over, with sweat on his brow his attention and thoughts went to wondering where David was and how could he kill him.

After one such victory the men of Ziph came to Saul and told him that David was once again come to their region. Once again Saul gathered his elite forces of three thousand men and moved without a day's rest to chase after David and his men.

David had quickly learned how to better distribute his troops and this time he would not be trapped on a hill to be surrounded. He positioned his men in groups of fifty scattered around the wilderness of Ziph and he himself was hidden on a hill with just fifty men with Abishai and Ahimelech the Hittite, two of his captains.

David watched from above as Saul set up camp with Abner at his side and his troops surrounding him. They were exhausted from war and their travels and got settled down quickly to rest for the night.

David knew the men of Ziph had again reported to Saul of his whereabouts. Again he was sad to be on the run avoiding daily threats and at the same time trying to encourage his followers. He whispered a melody under his breath and a song was born that went like this and became -

Psalm 54:

Save me, O God, by your name; vindicate me by your might. Hear my prayer, O God; listen to the words of my mouth. Strangers are attacking me; ruthless men seek my life—men without regard for God. *Selah*

Surely God is my help; the Lord is the one who sustains me. Let evil recoil on those who slander me; in your faithfulness destroy them. I will sacrifice a freewill offering to you I will praise your name, O Lord, for it is good. For he has delivered me from all my troubles, and my eyes have looked in triumph on my foes.

David's attitude toward Saul was conflicted to say the least. He honored the king. In his own heart he kept telling himself that he would never bring harm to the person of the king. This unnatural attitude regarding the man he knew was seeking to kill him was born out of David's own understanding of how a man of God would look at things.

David believed his life was in the hands of Yahweh. He trusted Yahweh for his own life in every situation. Since Yahweh had anointed him king, he knew that kingship would come and it was not something he would have to take.

But at the same time he could not just hand his life over to Saul. So, David concluded that it was his responsibility to stay alive and not foolishly expose himself to Saul, and at the same time, it was God's responsibility to take care of the timing of making David king.

Yet, here they were. Saul had gathered his troops and was hunting David. Rather than running away David argued within himself about what he should do. David could not help entertain conflicted thoughts. On one hand he thought, "Did God bring Saul here for me to kill him?"

And on the other hand he wondered, "But I love Saul and honor him as the king, how can I kill him? Since God put him on the throne how could I be the one to take him off?"

As David looked down on where Saul was going to sleep in a trench with Abner and others right next to him, he turned to his two captains and asked, "Who wants to go with me?" Abishai was first to jump up and volunteer to go with him.

At dark David and Abishai followed the path they had already determined was best. They knew where every sentry was and determined how to get to Saul with stealth. Abishai was getting excited again and whispering to David that once again Yahweh was delivering Saul into David's hands.

But David had made up his mind. He was going to once again prove to Saul that, while he could have killed Saul, he chose not to. Maybe this would finally convince Saul that he could stop worrying about David wanting the throne at any cost. Maybe Saul could finally see that David was willing to serve Saul without any inclination to be Saul's enemy.

From Saul's point of view things were also complicated. Saul was overly sensitive man, and responded to every reaction and judgment the people made about him. He concluded that he could not let David live. Saul knew that David's popularity was already higher than his own. The song sung almost daily by the people, would not go away, "Saul killed his thousands while David killed his tens of thousands."

It was as if a shroud covered the camp. Everything was pitch black and everyone was sound asleep. David and Abishai crept right up to where Saul was sleeping. Abishai was urging David to seize the moment and kill Saul.

In this setting the revelation and direction came to the heart of David about what he should do. David was able to grasp how the Holy Spirit was working in his own heart. It was as if a light shined down from heaven into the moment. He was filled with understanding of what would take place.

David said to Abishai, "Touch not God's anointed, whoever does will be held guilty and will deserve death himself." He went on to say, "One of three things will happen to Saul: God will take him, his day to die will come, or he will be killed in battle. This means I am not to have a hand in his death."

David said to Abishai, "Grab the king's spear and take his private water bottle and let's go."

When David and Abishai got back up to their camp they woke everyone and they got ready to move. At dawn David yelled out to Abner, "Are you the valiant man of the king? Aren't you supposed to protect him?" David continued his taunt, "If this is so, where is the king's sword and his private water bottle? You should die for not protecting the king."

Saul immediately recognized David's voice. Saul cried out, "Is that your voice my son, David?"

David answered, "It is my voice my king. Why are you pursuing me again? What have I done to deserve this?

David put forth an argument to Saul, "If God has stirred you up against me, let me make an offering unto the Lord so He will forgive me.

"If it is people stirring the king against me, then cursed are these people for they are driving me to serve other gods and to leave my inheritance in the land of Israel."

David went on, "Please don't take my blood on this field before the Lord. I am no more than a flea in the course of your life."

Saul was again smitten with shame. He called out to David, "I have sinned against you my son David, and no harm will come to you, so return to me. You could have taken my life and again you chose not to. I have been foolish and have made a grave error."

David still could not trust Saul. He could respect the office but he still doubted the man. David called out again, "Send one of your young men and I will return the king's special sword."

Then David chose to testify before the three thousand men of Saul, "Let it be remembered today that I spared the life of the king when that life had been put into my hands. May my life also be spared?"

Saul acknowledged, "Blessed are you my son, David. You will do great things and fulfill your destiny."

They each went their separate ways. Saul in sullen quietness rode his horse back to Gibeah. David, as he made his way a song came to his heart ending in these words (Psalm 57)

My heart is steadfast, O God, my heart is steadfast; I will sing and make music. Awake, my soul! Awake, harp and lyre! I will awaken the dawn.

I will praise you, O Lord, among the nations; I will sing of you among the peoples. For great is your love, reaching to the heavens; your faithfulness reaches to the skies.

Be exalted, O God, above the heavens; let your glory be over all the earth.

In his fear and pain for the unrighteous torment of living on the run, David found solace in the fact that he could rely upon the Living God to be his support. He spoke to his own heart telling himself to hold on, his help was in the name of the Lord.

David found that while his mind might play tricks on him, in worry and wonder, he could find stability in his heart. Where his mind might dwell on the worst that could happen, his heart would dwell on Yahweh.

It is true that as a man thinks in his heart so he is.

CHAPTER FOURTEEN

S aul's army could have concluded that peace was at hand for David. But the reality was that Saul had not called David to come to him face to face nor did Saul demonstrate any kind of meaningful reconciliation. David wisely read the shallow words from Saul and said to his close advisors, "He is going to try to kill me no matter what I do and no matter what he says."

Some might wonder why would not Yahweh protect David since David was the man He had anointed king? The fact was Yahweh was protecting David. Had Saul just charged after him he could have killed him. His main reason for not doing that was Saul was afraid of what the people would say if he outright killed David.

David needed to be cautious at every turn and not presume that Yahweh would shield him in acts of foolishness.

In David's heart he needed to be wise so that he might fulfill his side of the Promise of God and remain eligible to be that king.

David was a great organizer and had his followers broken down into groups of fifty with two groups working closely together. Joab headed a key group and was also a good adviser to David. He had a sense of the mood of the people and how best to handle them.

David was after all leading a ragtag group that had grown to over six hundred men. They continued in their daily training but provisions were becoming more difficult to find. To this point they had been running their sheep and goats and oxen with them. But this just slowed their ability to get away from the superior forces of Saul.

David met with Joab, Abishai, Adino, and Shammah and began to earnestly discuss their alternatives. In David's exasperation he did not seek word from Yahweh about the matter. But an outrageous idea came to him in the night and he sought the advice of his key men.

David said, "It seems certain to me that as long as Saul is alive I don't have a chance staying here in Israel. This idea came to me; what if we go to Gath and propose to Achish an alliance. He already knows that Saul considers me an enemy. If he would give us some land so we could water our flocks, and plant some food and sign a peace agreement with him and the other Philistines maybe we could just out live Saul's kingship."

Joab was the first to respond, "It is a brilliant idea. We could settle down and get our men proper training and we would not have to keep driving the women and children and cattle as we do now."

The Philistines were not all led by one man. There were regional kings that were in alliance with one another all under the umbrella of the name Philistines. David could tell from spies and reputations that Achish would be the most thoughtful and wise leader of the group. He had the respect of the other kings. Gath was in the lowlands and was very fertile and land was available to work without displacing anyone already there.

David took his followers lock stock and barrel, and marched into the region of Gath. Achish was well aware of the fracture of relationship between David and Saul and those marching were clearly not an army but refugees. So Achish gave David an audience to hear his proposal.

David bowed and said, "King Achish we come in peace. It is no longer possible for us to live in Israel and we seek a place to call our own. We don't want to intrude on you or this royal city. If you will just give us some place where water and farm land is available that will suit us. If Saul should attack we will not support him in any way. We will also give you offerings for any bounty we get as we go to other cities not allied with you."

Achish responded without hesitation, "Take your followers to Ziklag, that city will be just right for you and your needs. I agree with your terms so go in peace."

Achish was overjoyed to not have to fight David and Saul together. He was well aware of the bravery of David and the power of his leadership and that his followers would fight to the death. This new alliance was viewed as a weakening of Saul and therefore for the good of Achish and the other Philistine kings.

Word got back to Saul where David went to so he made no further attempts to search for and kill David. David ended up in this strange land for sixteen months free from Saul's torments.

As a part of the agreement between Achish and David, David's men were fully equipped with all the weapons of war that the Philistines had. Every man got a sword and shield, and armor, along with bows.

While David sought to take full advantage of the situation, it was a fearsome prospect for him to leave the land he had been anointed to rule and live for how long he did not know in this land of his enemies.

During this time David attacked some old enemies between there and Egypt. They fought against the Geshurites, the Gezrites, and the Amalekites. David took no prisoners. He killed every man, woman and child who was near the battlefield. He took all camels, sheep, oxen and donkeys. He also took all apparel, jewels and everything of value.

The only problem with these forays was that these were friends of Achish. While they were not wartime allies there were some agreements among them. When David returned to Gath with all the bounty, Achish smiled and said, "Well, it looks like you made a new road someplace?"

David lied in response, "I went over to the south of Judah and eliminated the Kenites and the Jerahmeelites and took this bounty."

David left no one alive where he had gone as he did not want any witnesses who would report to Achish. This might make Achish question his treaty with David if someone said, "David will do the same with you some day."

Of course Achish chose to believe David. The misdirection by David made Achish believe that David would be hated in Israel. It would make David all the more obligated to Achish and bring bounty to Achish for years to come.

During this season all the Philistine kings gathered together and decided to go to war with Israel. It seemed like an opportune time to the Philistines. They had heard of the departure of the great general David from Israel and surely Israel would be much weaker as a result of this defection. It was also known that many in Israel favored David so maybe; just maybe, they would be catching Israel at her weakest with these divisions in the ranks.

Achish met with David and gave him the news. He said, "David, you have been faithful sharing your bounty with me. As in evidence of your estrangement with Saul, you have destroyed some villages in Israel. Would you agree to go with me and fight against Saul?"

David replied without hesitation, "Yes, they want me to die anyway, so it might as well be in battle."

Achish liked David; he knew how smart and brave he was and that he was a great leader. His men followed him without question. So he asked David, "Will you fight at my side?

David again quickly replied, "It would be my honor to do so!"

As David walked away and back to his men he started wondering what he had just committed to. Would he really fight against his countrymen that he was destined to rule? At the same time, if he did not agree to go, what would Achish and the other Philistine kings do to him and his followers? They could crush him if they attacked.

David decided to let the events unfold and see what choices would be presented to him.

CHAPTER FIFTEEN

At the same time in Israel Saul was aware from his spies of the gathering armies. He was very upset for since Samuel had died, Saul had nowhere to turn to seek God's direction. As the battle day got closer Saul saw with his own eyes the gathering of the host of the Philistines, and they seemed to fill the mountains and plains with soldiers.

Saul's heart grew faint; he was after all not a brave man in any sense of the word. So without Samuel Saul sought Yahweh by himself. God did not answer, or so it seemed to Saul for he could not understand him if he had.

He called for a priest who brought out the Urim (the charm used to discern an action) and still no word. He called the prophets from Samuel's school of the prophets and still no word. As a last resort he called his servants and asked the whereabouts of the woman with the "familiar spirit."

All witches and soothsayers had been banished and forbidden to seek dark spirits when Samuel was alive. Samuel had pushed Saul to banish such activity. There were few secrets in Israel and Saul's servants were aware of a woman who still practiced the dark arts. They spoke up and told Saul there was such a woman at a place called Endor.

Saul disguised himself and went a day and part of a night to see the woman. He entered her tent and asked her to call up the spirit of the man he needed counsel from. She did not know she was speaking to the king. But she still was reluctant and she responded, "You know that

Saul has made a law that those with familiar spirits and wizards are no longer allowed in the land of Israel. Are you trying to trick me?"

Without divulging who he was he swore to her, "As the Lord liveth there shall be no harm or punishment come to you for this thing."

She thought he carried himself as someone who must be rich, with such an entourage and fine horses. So she responded, "Who shall I bring up?"

Saul said, "Bring up to me Samuel!"

She started speaking magical words and incantations, with incense burning. This went on for half the hour and Saul, with his armour bearers waiting outside, just sat there and watched and wondered at all the gibberish.

Suddenly the woman saw someone start to manifest out of the dark and she cried out, "Why have you deceived me? You are Saul!"

He said to her, "Don't be afraid, tell me what you see?

She said, "I saw gods ascending out of the earth."

He said, "What form is he or what does he look like?"

She said, "He is an old man and he is covered with a mantle or a cloak."

Saul could not see who it was for himself, but he concluded that it must be Samuel. Saul got down on his hands and knees with his face to the ground.

Through the woman, in a voice different from hers she said, "Why have you brought me up here?"

Saul responded, "I am in great distress; the Philistines are marching against us to make war. God has departed from me and will not answer no matter how I ask him. I have prayed and nothing. He has not given me any dreams, nor have any of his prophets had a word for me. That is why I have called for you that you may tell me what to do."

Through the witch the voice spoke again, "If the Lord has departed from you then why are you asking me? It seems clear He has become you enemy?"

She then continued, "The Lord has rent the kingdom out of your hand and given it to your young general David. Again, the Lord has done this because you would not obey him and did not kill Amalek as you had been clearly instructed."

She went on in a tone becoming more serious and dark, "The Lord hath done this thing today, He will deliver all of Israel into the hands of the Philistines tomorrow and you and your sons will join me!"

An agony fell upon Saul as if he were dead. He fell to the floor and did not move for over an hour. The news was devastating. What Saul knew to be true in his heart was now at hand. He had feared this moment and expected it, but had hoped against hope that somehow he would be forgiven and that judgment of God could be delayed longer, if not forgotten.

The witch of Endor was filled with fear at Saul's response to the session. She began to plead with him, saying that she had simply done what he had demanded. But as he lay on her tent floor, hardly moving at all, she further pleaded, "Let me prepare you some food so you may regain your strength."

Her entreaties reached him and he listened to her in his great sadness, he got up from the floor and sat upon her bed. He sat in a daze as she arose, killed a calf, made bread, and cooked and prepared a meal for him as these words hung over his head.

After eating the prepared meal, Saul and his entourage left in the stillness of the night.

CHAPTER SIXTEEN

The Philistines were gathered in array and preparing for battle. King Achish came up behind the army with his contingent of soldiers. David and his men were at the end of this contingent. The princes of the Philistines saw David and became furious. They confronted King Achish and said, "Is not this the great general of Saul?"

King Achish replied, "He has been with me over one year. He has been faithful to me and has brought me bounty from his exploits. He and Saul are enemies and he has promised to fight at my side. I trust him completely."

The princes' response was quick and vocal, "No, we will not have him behind us. He is an Israelite and in the heat of battle, we cannot trust that he will not turn against us. It has been rumored that he will succeed as king someday, so no — send him back."

King Achish relented. He came back to David and apologized to him saying, "The other kings will not allow you to come with us, so return to Ziklag."

David turned his men around and began the march back. He was having second thoughts himself about going to battle against his own people. Perhaps there would have been a way that he could have helped the people of Israel and once and for all defeat these miserable Philistines. Among the Philistines he had been keeping up appearances that he was against Saul and at least King Achish was still on his side.

As they slowly made their way back to Ziklag they looked over the horizon and wondered as they saw smoke coming from the city.

When they got closer they saw the city was deserted. Every woman and child and animal was gone! As they walked throughout the city they saw there were no bodies and saw nothing dead. They found a flag bearing the banner of the Amalekites.

The Amalekites had exacted retribution for David's attacks on them. As the men of David walked the streets a great agony came over them. They wept in sadness. Here they were, they had been rejected by Saul, now they were being rejected by the Philistines, and now everything they owned was taken from them.

In small groups many started for the first time to complain about David's leadership. There was even talk of stoning David. His key leaders Abishai and Joab tried to keep the talk down, saying it was not all David's fault. David walked off dazed and felt more alone than he ever had in his life.

He did only what he knew to do. He turned to Yahweh and began to worship him. He had long ago found his only comfort in impossible situations was to worship God with all his heart and with all his soul. Something remarkable took place as David began to worship. David raised his arms to the sky. He sang songs of praise as words flowed from his heart. At the same time he sensed a response in his heart from heaven. It was as if he was in heaven and could understand the mind of God. At this moment of ultimate loneliness, the Holy Spirit made himself known to David. A sense of comfort began to flood over him like a wave in the sea.

David spoke to his own heart the words he believed he heard in heaven. He told himself to take courage, that Yahweh was with him and would make a way where there was no way.

In the ruined city everyone had cried until there were no more tears. Anger was on the surface but David came forth in the power of the Holy Spirit and called for Abiathar the priest to seek the counsel of the Lord.

Abiathar brought the ephod (the prayer cloth of the priest) and David asked Abiathar to ask the Lord, "Shall I pursue this troop that has taken all that we have, including wives and children and animals, and shall I overtake them?"

The Lord responded immediately through Abiathar, "Yes, pursue them, and you shall overtake them AND you shall recover everyone and everything that has been taken!"

David stood before the leaders and those gathered around and repeated the words of the Lord. When he spoke in this manner his men thought an angel was speaking. He spoke with such conviction and authority the likes of which his men had never heard.

It became the mantra of the march as the men found new courage and hope: "We shall pursue. We shall overtake. We shall recover all." They kept repeating these words and their faith grew with each step and word.

In pursuit they came to a brook called Besor. To get to Ziklag it had taken three days journey. Now they were another day marching with little food and little water. Out of the six hundred men with David, two hundred could go no further for exhaustion. There was minor disgruntlement from the four hundred that continued on, but onward they went.

They found a young Egyptian boy who appeared to be dying by the side of the road. David gave him nourishment and asked him who he was. He had been a servant to the Amalekites and became sick three days ago. So his master left him. He told David about the cities they had plundered including Ziklag.

David then asked him, "Can you take me to where they are?"

The young man replied, "Swear to me that you won't kill me and that you will not return me to my master and I will show you where they have gone."

The Amalekites, knowing the Philistines and Israel were at war, were in no hurry to get anywhere. David and his men closed in stealthily to see them over the hill. They were in a party mood, dancing, drinking and in celebration. The spoils of war had been great and they had no idea that anyone would be following them. The party had gone on until almost dawn and now they were lying around in drunken stupors with no sentries for warning.

David and his men arrayed against this company as if they were in an all out war. They separated them from their supplies and armaments. They began killing them methodically as it took much time for the Amalekites to wake up and realize they were being attacked.

David left not a man standing alive anywhere in the camp. He led his men in pursuit, they had overtaken this enemy and they recovered alive every woman and child and animal. David got his two wives back, for he had married another after Abigail. In addition to their own goods, they also got all the other spoil the Amalekites had taken from Judah and the region where Caleb's family had been. Their bounty then doubled in size with more herds than they ever had before.

As they returned to Ziklag they came again to the brook Besor. The two hundred who had been unable to go forward were there waiting. There was much resentment toward them. Some of the four hundred spoke up and said, "We will not give them any of the spoil except they can each have their own wives and children."

David said, "Wait! These spoils are what the Lord has given us. He preserved us and delivered these enemies into our hands. It is to be a law in the land, that we all share equally in the spoils, both they that fought and they that stayed by the stuff."

Reluctantly they all agreed for they all acknowledged that God had dropped the enemy in their lap and that it was no great feat to win that battle.

The spoils were so bountiful, that David carefully gathered offerings to send to various tribal elders throughout Israel. He sent them to the elders at Judah, Bethel, Ramoth, Jattir, Aroer, and eight other cities as well as to Hebron the capital of Judah.

David as usual kept an eye on the future believing that sowing some bounty today would bring great returns in the future when the help of tribal leaders might be needed.

CHAPTER SEVENTEEN

The Philistines were now highly organized. They took up positions that enabled them to come at Saul and his army from three different directions. But the tribes of Israel were in disarray. No one had seen or heard from Saul for almost a week since he disappeared. His lack of direction and uncertainty in the orders he left caused much confusion among the troops.

Yes, he had three thousand well-trained soldiers equipped with swords, some armour and bows and arrows. But the balance of his army was not well disciplined and not very well equipped. They were a volunteer army at best. Yes, they would follow orders, but what is the point when no orders were coming forth. Consequently, there was much fear evident.

Saul found his way back to Gibeah traveling a day and a half on horseback and in disguise. It was a hard journey and he could not share with Jonathan or even Abner where he had been or what he had been doing.

Saul had two of his other sons there on the battlefield, Abinadab and Malchishua, and they also came to meet together with Saul. They quickly brought him up to date on how the enemy was arrayed and what they would have to do to take on an assault. Things were bleak at best. There was little faith in the camp. The past few days of watching the enemy take up positions to their advantage were bringing more doubt daily to the men of Israel.

It was as if the Philistines had waited for Saul to return to the battlefront. The very next day they came charging at every commander

Israel had. The resistance was virtually nonexistent. In fact, the men of Israel took off in five different directions, some even going back across the Jordan River to get away.

The scouts of the Philistines were accurate in identifying where Saul and his sons were. They overran their positions and killed them without mercy. The sons died first and Saul was trying to escape. First one arrow then another arrow hit him. The first one got him in the shoulder, but the second one got him in the back. He was bleeding and getting weaker but he was not sure he would die right away.

The last thing Saul wanted was to allow his enemies a chance to torture him. With both arrows still in him as he fell from his horse, he called out to his armour bearer. The armour bearer came near with tears in his eyes. He loved his king.

Saul said, "Take your sword and kill me quickly, I do not want to give these uncircumcised heathens the opportunity to abuse me."

The armour bearer, with tears streaming down his face, confessed that he could not do it. How could he take the life of his king whom he had pledged to protect with his life?

Saul then fell on his own sword. The armour bearer witnessed this last brave act and he, too, took his own life.

The Philistines were close on the trail of getting to Saul. They found him while the body was still warm and they began to dance and sing because truly the battle was won. They cut off the head of Saul, took his sword and the bodies of his sons and carried them forth to put on display before their own gods at the city of Bethshan. They dedicated the armour to the patron goddess Astarte. Then they took the mutilated bodies and hung them on the wall at Bethshan.

All the men of Israel left the cities and villages and fled for the wilderness hiding in fear. News traveled fast and word got out quickly that Saul and three of his sons died with him. The Philistines meanwhile occupied almost all of the country and the nation of Israel, so recently united, was broken asunder.

The men of Jabesh-gilead heard how Saul's remaining body was left in the field. They travelled all night and at dawn arrived at Bethshan. They took down the bodies and brought them back to Jabesh. There they burned the bodies and buried them under the largest and oldest tree in the territory.

Then the men of Jabesh fasted and mourned for Saul and his sons for seven days to honor them in their death. It had been Saul who broke a siege against Jabesh twenty years earlier and the people here held him in the highest regard.

Abner, the key general for Saul escaped. He understood Saul's ambivalence better than anyone. Saul's unexplained disappearance before the battle had prompted Abner to make his own contingency plans. He had two lieutenants who would follow his orders without hesitation so horses and provisions were hidden and at the ready when the expected happened.

There was a fourth son of Saul and his name was Ishbosheth. Abner installed him as king immediately, in a city named Mahanaim. Abner was not a fool and he certainly was aware that David was around and, now that Saul was gone, he was sure David would make a move to replace Saul.

For all Abner knew David would kill him as well as any other of Saul's captains as well as any remaining members of the household. So Abner moved quickly to gain support of the population before David could make this kind of a move.

At the coronation of Ishbosheth, Abner made him king over Gilead, Jezreel, Ephraim, the Ashurites, Benjamin and all of the northern tribes of Israel. He purposely avoided the southern tribes as they were of the family of David, so this approach made the most political sense.

There was another political consideration in the matter. The Philistines had defeated Israel. Consequently, they would be an occupying force that would expect monthly and annual bounty. They would demand a portion of the harvest and of the herds and any sales made through the caravans that travelled from the Crescent down to Egypt.

The Philistines, therefore, favored splitting the kingdom of Israel, diminishing the threat that they might organize again to rise up and rebel. So they allowed and encouraged Ishbosheth and made treaty with him as long as he would meet their taxation demands.

Both internal and external forces seemed to facilitate the coronation of Ishbosheth quickly after the loss of Saul.

CHAPTER EIGHTEEN

While the battle had raged against Saul, David and his men returned in victory over the Amalekites to Ziklag. They had been back only two days when an out of breath messenger ran towards David.

The messenger's clothes were torn, hanging down in strips. He had dirt plastered on his head, a sign of defeat and humility, as he fell at the feet of David.

The boy called out and said he had escaped from the camp of Israel.

David said, "What news do you bring from the battle?"

He answered, "I happened to be there in the heat of their battle. Saul was wounded with two arrows sticking out of him and the enemy in close pursuit. Saul called out to me to come kill him to spare him from being abused by the Philistines who were on their way up the hill."

David said, "What happened next?"

The boy had rehearsed his story to gain position. He had been nearby when Saul asked his armour bearer to kill him. So he thought he would take advantage of the results and come to David for reward.

The boy said, "I was sure he would not survive, so I stood over him and slew him with his own sword. Then I took his crown and his bracelet and brought them to you my lord."

David began tearing his clothes and weeping for his friend Jonathan and for King Saul. It was a sad day for David that an enemy of Israel had defeated the army of Israel and their king and generals.

David asked him, "Where is your family from?"

The boy answered, "I am an Amalekite."

David said, "Weren't you afraid to stretch your hand out to kill the Lord's anointed?"

David called one of his young men and said, "Kill this fool, who with his own mouth testified that he killed the anointed of the Lord."

He was struck down before a protest could escape his lips.

David began a lament. His first thoughts were sorely conflicted. He lost his best friend in life in Jonathan, who had been closer to him than a brother. They had dreamed of the future together in leading the Nation under Yahweh. This loss to David was very personal and recovery would be difficult. He would fulfill his promises to Jonathan and take care of Jonathan's survivors. But deep pain found a place in David's heart.

The loss of King Saul also presented some deep emotions in David's heart. For more than ten years David had lived every day with the threat lurking that the king sought hard to kill him. Saul's death lifted a burden on David's heart whereby he suddenly felt free.

This new sense of freedom filled his heart, a freedom that was to play an important part in his future.

But David hated the idea that an enemy had killed the king. If David was going to become king then these events certainly highlighted the dangers which accompanied the great opportunity.

 David, former shepherd, renowned warrior, and emerging great general, also recognized the political ramifications of the sudden loss of the king over the nation.

As David contemplated these events, he returned to his first source of strength. He let his emotions find expression as he turned his heart to God in worship. He had found his way back to centering his life in song and praise.

David began singing as he got out his chordophone,

"How the mighty are fallen and the weapons of war perished."

He went on, **"The beauty of Israel is slain upon the high places, and how the mighty are fallen."**

"Ye mountains of Gilboa should no longer have dew or any rain. For there the shield of the mighty has vilely been cast away. It was as if the shield of Saul had not been anointed with oil.

"The bow of Jonathan turned not back (he did not run away) and the sword of Saul returned not empty.

"Saul and Jonathan were lovely and pleasant in their lives and in their deaths they were not divided. They were swifter than eagles and stronger than lions.

 "Ye daughters of Israel, weep over Saul who clothed you in scarlet, and provided you with ornaments of gold.

"I am distressed for you, my brother Jonathan, you have been pleasant to me and your love was wonderful, passing the love of women.

"How are the mighty fallen, and the weapons of war perished!"

CHAPTER NINETEEN

Within days a new reality dawned on David. His mind went back to the time that Samuel had anointed him king. After his tears dried he began to consider what needed to happen next.

He knew there were survivors in the family of Saul. Jonathan had several brothers and David was not sure how they would react. The last thing he wanted to do was kill Ishbosheth who might well lay claim to the throne.

It was a time to be careful. He wanted to be king and believed he should position himself to allow that to happen. At the same time he did not want to use force to gain the throne. The tribes tended to have long memories. While there was a desire to stand united — at the same time they valued their independence.

So the challenge was to walk the fine line between showing power and being very careful how that power was used. David had learned how to lead a group of fiercely independent men over the last few years. They were from all the tribes so he had come to know and understand some of the history and tendencies of each tribe.

He did not think it would be the "will of Yahweh" if he took the kingship by force and he wasn't sure he could at this time anyway. He did not have enough men to win an all-out battle if the tribes came together against him.

Again, he turned to his first source, asking the Lord, "Should I leave Ziklag and return to my homeland in Judah?"

The Lord said, "Go up."

David said, "To which city should I go?"

The Lord said, "Return to Hebron."

David took his two wives, Ahinoam the Jezreelitess, and Abigail, Nabal's wife, with him and went up to Hebron. He went to his men and their families and gave them the news that they were going to Hebron. They all agreed and took their possessions, their herds, and families and came to live in Hebron.

Hebron was a city with a special history. Only two men travelling with the children of Israel in the wilderness under the leadership of Moses had survived the forty year journey. The two men were known as men of faith with a "different spirit" about them than others on the journey. They believed God! No matter what God said or did they agreed. The two men were Joshua and Caleb.

After Israel had returned to the Promised Land, Caleb had asked Joshua (God's newly appointed leader of Israel), if he could have the land of Hebron for his heritage.

At the time, Hebron was the home of giants among the people. But Caleb, the great man of faith, claimed the land and took it by force. With a sword in his hand, he led his tribe to conquer the land of the giants even though he was already eighty five years old.

So it was in this same kind of faith that David led the tribe of Judah to their newly named capital of the Southern Tribes.

When they settled in, the elders of the tribe, led by Ahithophel, and the men of Judah came to David and "anointed" him as their king. They had always identified with David during his conflict with Saul. David was their own hero and they did not want to identify with Abner and Ishbosheth in any way. David was now the king of Judah which included the two southern tribes.

Ahithophel came to David's side and became a close counselor on political matters. He was respected throughout Israel and his political counsel wise beyond words. He could read the hearts of the tribe and for that matter, the heart of the nation.

Ahithophel and David had daily meetings for months, discussing the power and responsibilities of a king. At the same time, David had many of his own ideas. Being king was his destiny and he had thought over many of these matters for years.

In Ahithophel's thinking the role of a king was first to give security to all tribes of Israel. When one is attacked, they are all attacked and must respond as one. David of course had discovered over the years that troop training and discipline were of paramount importance in building a successful army.

David learned from Moses how to set up a chain of command. He learned how to organize captains over thousands, over hundreds, over fifties and over tens. He had many months of thinking and planning on how to organize and train troops and approach battle.

The king had the authority to conscript the sons of the tribes as he saw fit. David's plans were not tied to Hebron, even though it was where he was first anointed to be king. David saw this as a stepping stone, as did Ahithophel, and they were discussing plans well beyond the present.

After being anointed King of Judah there was another issue David needed to cover carefully. He contacted King Achish and told him of the developments. Because his "enemy," King Saul was killed, David "wanted" to return to his home in Judah.

He did not ask for permission, but he informed him and invited him to his coronation in Hebron. The Philistines, in a sense, "permitted" David to rule in Hebron as long as the other ten tribes remained separate. It was again in the best interests of the Philistines to keep the nation of Israel divided.

In addition, Ahithophel told David of the kindness of the men of Jabesh-gilead, how they preserved the honor of Israel in recovering Saul and Jonathan and his brothers from the display in Bethshan. He advised David to send messengers to the men of Jabesh thanking them and offering an alliance with them for the honor they showed to the fallen king.

David also let them know that Judah made David king over Judah, hoping that this would motivate them to align with him. For the next seven years and six months David reigned as king over Judah in Hebron. His reign was popular and noted by all the tribes of Israel.

Meanwhile, Ishbosheth reigned in Mahanaim but he ruled for only two years. He was very much like his father. He suffered with insecurities and mood swings leading to depression.

The Northern tribes were back to fending for themselves without much of a leader to hold them together.

Over the last few years Joab increased his position of leadership in David's army. He had been instrumental in pursuing and overtaking the Amalekites and he was always available to David whenever David sought counsel or help in any way.

Abner sent a message to David suggesting a meeting of representatives of the two kings to begin negotiations for cooperation against their common occupying force. Since the Philistines had beaten Saul, they occupied Israel because there was no organized army to drive them out.

Abner and Joab met, with a set number of five hundred guards each to begin discussions. They met at the pool at Gibeon which was a neutral territory and one gathered on one side of the pool and one on the other side.

Abner, having brought out his guards from the best of the trained full time army, suggested that each side let twelve young men arise "to play." His word choice was noted but hidden intention was obvious.

Representing Ishbosheth were twelve young men from the tribe of Benjamin, the family of Saul. Representing David was twelve of his servants who had walked with him from the cave at Adullan. David's men arose and met the other twelve, with no game in mind. Rather as one, each of David's men seized his opponent's head and thrust a sword in his side. At this sudden turn of events the rest of the men of Abner rose to fight, as did the men with Joab.

The battle was ugly and bloody, but Abner and the men of Israel were soundly beaten that day. They allowed Abner to retreat, as he had done before in battle when he had left Saul to his death. But there was one young man who refused to let Abner slink away. His name was Asahel, the youngest brother of Joab. Asahel was a messenger, not a warrior, who could run three hours straight without stopping to get a message from a battle field.

Asahel ran after Abner who was on his horse and would not let him out of his sight. Abner became irritated with the pursuit and told Asahel to don some armour and defend himself in battle or go home. Asahel refused, he was not a warrior, but he would not stop the chase.

Finally, Abner took his spear and smote Asahel under the fifth rib and the spear came out his back. Abner left him lying there for all who passed by to see. There were others in pursuit beside Asahel and when they arrived at the place he died they stood there mute. They all knew Asahel was not a warrior, but a messenger, and represented no threat to Abner. Therefore, his kill was abhorred – and Asahel being the brother of Joab and Abishai meant they knew an honor was at stake.

Abner went to a nearby hill and the children of Benjamin gathered with him as one. When Joab arrived at the gathering Abner called out to him, "Shall the sword devour forever? You know as well as I, if the two sides do not come to some form of agreement bitterness will be the end of us all. We are brothers after all is said and done."

Joab sensed the mood of the plea. It was true that an all-out war among the children of Israel would make no sense. In any event, David was not there and Joab did not have authority to start a war with the northern tribes. So Joab took out his trumpet and blew the sound to return and everyone quit fighting and began their journey home. Joab resisted the demand for vengeance rising in his heart and knew there would be another day.

Abner and his men walked all night to get back to Mahanaim; they had lost three hundred and sixty men that day fighting the men of Judah. Joab and his men returned having lost only nineteen men and his little brother Asahel. Joab would always remember Abner for killing his harmless brother.

He carried his brother and buried him in his hometown of Bethlehem and then walked all night to get back to Hebron and report to David.

Despite how tired he was, Joab reported immediately because he knew David wanted the news quickly. Joab reported that an agreement had not been on the agenda for he assumed his men were stronger and more skilled than David's. They found out quickly though that David's training and quality of fighters far surpassed the training of Abner's men.

There was to be a long, drawn out war between the house of Saul and the house of David. But the war was not declared formally. It was made up of skirmishes fought with a few men at a time so as not to incite all-out civil war. The antagonism was evident, but Abner and Ishbosheth were not confident after the confrontational loss of over three hundred of their men to the loss of less than twenty of David's men.

CHAPTER TWENTY

With so much freedom of thought and no longer on the run, David had time on his hands he had not ever experienced before. He expanded his worship time with Yahweh. He gathered singers and musicians and held a worship service every morning and evening.

But he also began taking more interest in women.

He had come to Hebron with two wives and found a third wife named Maacah a daughter of Talmai the king of Geshur. Political weddings were common to assure peace.

Maacah bore David his third son and his name was Absalom. Geshur was located in Syria and David sought alliances with some of his surrounding enemies. An alliance with Geshur would give him a buffer geographically against the Ammonites who continually were at odds with Israel.

Maccah was gorgeous to look at. She had a beautiful body and an unusual head of hair. It was very long, falling below her knees, and it was very thick and had to be combed out every morning by a handmaiden.

David had an eye for women and, since he was not under constant threat and not fighting major wars, the pressures were less and he had time for them. Not only did he have an eye for women, he had an eye for beautiful women.

One of his "boyhood" friends from his days as a shepherd, named Hushai shared this bent toward women. So David often used him to scout for the "beauties" and with approval from David, Hushai would invite the women to meet David.

Hushai kept the confidence of the king and protected him around the women of the house. No woman, including any of his wives, could walk into the presence of the king without approval of Hushai.

David then acquired three more wives in Hebron giving him a total of six wives. They gave him six more children while he reigned in Hebron.

In the Northern ten tribes under the reign of Ishbosheth, Abner was clever and made his position stronger everyday with influence and power. He took care of the men surrounding the king and they looked to his leadership. But he was not interested in making decisions for the good of the people. He was greedy and underhanded and in this position sought only his self-interest.

In the past, Abner had been fascinated by one of Saul's concubines and found reasons to be in her presence as often as he could. Following Saul's death he decided to take her for his own. Upon learning this, Ishobeth said to him, "Who do you think you are taking a concubine of Saul to your bed?"

Abner turned on Ishbosheth in rage and vengeance and challenged him back, "Who do you think you are? If it weren't for me you would be dead and David would reign over the entire country. It is amazing that I did not deliver you into his hands to die, and you dare to challenge me about some woman?"

Abner threatened further, "I think I am going to change my allegiance and switch to David and translate the kingdom from the house of Saul to the house of David. Then David can rule from Dan even to Beersheba.

Ishbosheth stood mute for he knew the threats were real. Without Abner Ishbosheth had nothing and he knew it.

Thereafter their positions were clearly understood. Ishbosheth was king but Abner ruled.

Eventually Abner decided diplomacy might be better with David. After all, every time they fought with David's men they lost and there was no way Abner could rally all the volunteer army of Israel behind him to fight against David. David still had many friends throughout the tribes. Abner was clever and sent a message to David saying, "I will make a treaty with you and I will work to bring all of Israel under your ruler ship."

David had a long memory. He refused to negotiate with Abner directly so he sent his reply to Ishbosheth. He said, "I will enter into a treaty but I want one thing. You will not see my face unless you bring me Michal, Saul's daughter. I paid for her and she is mine."

Ishbosheth did not hesitate. He knew his brother Jonathan and David were best friends. Jonathan had told him what a great man David was. Ishbosheth, with Abner at his side, began to wonder if he would not be better under David himself.

Ishbosheth's father had given Michal to Phaliel to be his wife. Ishbosheth took her from Phaliel and sent her to David. Phaliel wept like a child and attempted to follow her on her journey to David but Abner stopped him and sent him home.

Abner had contacted all the elders of Israel and held a secret meeting with them. They all knew their new king was lacking and Abner started the meeting by saying, "In the past you sought for David to be over you as king. Even the Lord has spoken that He would save his people of Israel out of the hand of the Philistines and out of the hand of all our enemies through David as king. Now is the time to make him your king."

So Abner discussed it with Benjamin and gained his agreement. He then went to David at Hebron to tell him of the agreement of all the elders as well as the house of Benjamin. With the tradition of killing off all the relatives of the previous king, the house of Benjamin had the most to lose. But all agreed to make David the king.

Abner came with twenty men and David ordered a feast of celebration for them. During the feast Abner rose and told them all was ready for David to be king over the whole nation. There was joy in Hebron and David sent Abner away in peace after receiving words that all was in order for him to be king.

Just after Abner's departure, Joab arrived with a bounty of riches from recent victories. He inquired about the celebration and learned of Abner's visit and agreement with David.

He then went to King David and challenged him, "What have you done? Abner came to you and you sent him away in peace. You know he came to deceive you and he came to see our operations here and to see how we come and go in our security."

Joab, with a heart filled with vengeance, was unable to grasp the significance of the moment. He missed completely the fact that David had just arranged to be king without further bloodshed.

Joab left without satisfaction. He sent messengers to Abner and told him David had more to discuss so please return. They caught up to him at the well of Sirah.

David did not know of any of this. When Abner returned, Joab met him at the gate and took him to a small meeting place to speak to him quietly.

Without warning or words Joab took out his blade and stabbed Abner under the fifth rib, pulling the blade with force tearing his heart, spleen, and into his lungs. He died without a word to satisfy the vengeance for the blood of Asahel, Joab's brother.

Upon learning of Abner's death, David was enraged. Just as all Israel readied to gather in peace under David's leadership, murder threatened to muddy the waters.

Joab had taken his vengeance at the worst possible time.

David had to react quickly and decisively to preserve the peace and make sure that this event would not interfere with the agreements entered into.

David published his sadness over the death of Abner. He openly declared he had nothing to do with it and that the blood of Abner was on the house of Joab.

David went on with this curse to Joab and his posterity, "Let there not fail from the house of Joab one that hath an issue, or is a leper, or is crippled, or that dies by the sword or one that does not have enough food to eat."

David then forced Joab and all the people to go into mourning over Abner and he ordered a large processional throughout Hebron for the funeral of Abner. David lamented over Abner and even wrote a song for him.

His open mourning was for all to see and the sincerity of it reached the hearts of the people. David fasted all day and the people tried to get him to eat but he refused to eat until the sun went down.

All the people took notice of David and it pleased them how humble and caring he was. It was broadcast around the nation that David had nothing to do with the death of Abner. After all Abner did have many friends in many places so David could ill afford offending those allies of Abner that he sought to win over.

David made the point loud and clear by saying that, "The Lord shall reward the doer of evil according to his wickedness."

The relationship between Joab and David never recovered. Even though Joab remained in the inner circle of all battle plans, the breach would never be fully repaired. He certainly was a warrior and outstanding tactician. But in terms of being a political counselor or for that matter a counselor of any significance, Joab would never have that privilege again.

What he did jeopardized the very moment of ascension that was due David, and only because David could reach the hearts of the people was he able to survive the blunder of Joab.

This was a tense time for the entire nation. Ishbosheth heard the news that Abner was dead. If the man who in effect controlled his life was killed what would happen to him? He was not a brave man in the first place.

Ishbosheth had two loyal captains in spite of Abner's control. They were as fearful as he was. Their names were Baanah and Recheb. They were also of the house of Benjamin and feared the uncertainty of what David would do when he became king.

There was another player in the historical drama to consider. Jonathan had a son and his name was Mephibosheth. He had been only five years old when his father died. When news came that Jonathan and Saul had been killed, his nurse fled with the baby in her arms to save him. She fell in her haste and the baby Mephibosheth became lame from that day and for the rest of his life.

The two "loyal" captains came to Ishbosheth in the heat of the day. They found him lying on his bed. It seemed the depressions that came on his father also afflicted him. They were ushered into the bedroom and left alone with him. They killed him as he lay in bed. They stabbed him under the fifth rib – into the heart. They cut off his head and in the dark of the night they fled across the plains carrying the head of the king.

They arrived two days later to meet David at Hebron. Because they had been known to be captains and "loyal" to Ishbosheth they were allowed in the presence of David.

They bowed before him and said, "Behold the head of Ishbosheth, the son of Saul, your enemy, who sought to kill you. The Lord has avenged our king David this day of Saul and his seed."

David looked at the head dangling from the hand of Baanah and in a quiet rage said, "The Lord has redeemed my soul out of all adversity. When one came telling me that Saul was dead, thinking he was giving me good news, I took him and killed him on the spot.

"How much more will I do to wicked men that have killed a righteous man in his own house and in his own bed? Now I require your blood and take away you both from off the face of the earth!"

David's men immediately struck the two men down. Then David commanded that their hands and feet be cut off and hung over the pool in Hebron as a testimony of justice that again David had nothing to do with the death of Ishbosheth. He took the head of Ishbosheth and buried him with Abner in Hebron, giving him honor in his untimely death.

David continued to be careful in all public appearances. He did not want to appear to be seizing control or forcing his kingship on anyone. Since the day he was anointed king as a teenager it could almost be said he avoided being king rather than he tried to become king.

David had an underlying belief that if Yahweh wanted him to be king then he would live as if he was forcing Yahweh to make it happen rather than ever be accused of making it happen himself.

CHAPTER TWENTY ONE

D avid chose the high ground during the void of leadership in the northern tribes of Israel. He expanded his rule in Judah and his army trained daily. They found more recruits and continued their success by seeking out villages throughout the lands of their enemies, conquering them and bringing back the spoils of war.

From time to time he would send gifts to elders in the northern tribes, mentioning that the bounty were spoils from defeated enemies. He made virtually no trips to the north during this time. He made the decision not to aggressively campaign for the office of king.

Ahithophel and David had a long discussion about kingship. David said, "I believe that kingship over Israel is only Yahweh's to give." He then told how he had been "anointed king of Israel" by Samuel almost twenty years prior. This was the first time anyone outside his family knew that anointing had taken place.

Ahithophel was excited to hear this family secret. He had always known in his own heart that David had a special destiny. So Ahithophel led the house of Judah in recognizing David's kingship when David was celebrating his 30th birthday.

David went on to rule in Hebron for seven years and six months.

It was a good time for David. The Philistines were well aware of the political upheaval in Israel. Ishbosheth had lasted only two years, so David lasted five and one half years longer in Judah. The Philistines elected not to launch any major all out campaigns against Israel. They were happy with the taxes they were collecting and there was no sense in pushing too hard. But, the taxation strategy of the Philistines did squeeze a little more each year from their subjects.

They were very aware of the prowess of David and his tenure in Judah served their purposes. They had a taste of how powerful Israel could be under the right leadership, so the political decision was to keep Israel divided. They basically avoided invading the Southern Tribes and put the most pressure at the weakest areas in the North.

The elders of the Northern ten tribes knew that they had gone backwards without a king. They were frustrated to say the least and kept meeting in small groups seeking solutions.

The Philistines still attacked from time to time when they just wanted "more." The pressure seemed to grow with each year more of their sons dying in battle. More and more crops were lost or stolen and economic growth and expansion were never possible as long as they were under the thumb of the Philistines.

After their fourth annual elders meeting following the death of Ishbosheth they began serious discussion about making David king over all of Israel. There was some concern. The House of Benjamin wondered whether he would kill all the men of Benjamin. This was a real question, as this was the house Saul had come from. They had no way to know if David would or would not kill all the family members of the former king — the common method for eliminating any possible claims to the throne.

They were also concerned where the capital city would be. Saul had ruled from Gibeah. Hebron was quite far south in the land and would make it hard for a king to stay informed of the needs of those tribes to the north.

But in prayer and finally with 100% agreement, the elders sent a message to David requesting a meeting with him in Hebron.

They had a prepared speech in which they acknowledged, "David we are of your bone and of your flesh. In the time past while Saul was king you were the leader of our army that brought victories to us. In addition, the Lord had said to you that you would feed his people and that you would be our captain."

It was interesting to David that they were repeating what they thought the Lord had said to him.

So the elders stood together united and requested David to be their king. It was a sovereign moment in the life of David. He would become king without having to kill one person. He did not attack anyone of the household of Saul. He did not seek to eliminate any competition.

He made no campaigning efforts for the position. Yes, he had kept communications open, but there were no overt appeals to make him king. David used no underhanded means to gain this recognition as the new king.

In another meeting with Ahithophel he said, "This proves to me that this was the work of Yahweh. It is now established in my own heart and mind that the foundation of my position is based on the will of God."

"I will not be required to serve any man, but as king my focus is to serve God. I will not be captive to the whims of men nor forced to keep people happy. I am free to serve with my only obligations being to the Lord."

Ahithophel was amazed at the insight and focus of this man. He responded to David, "Now I see the extent of the faith you have in life.

Not only are you a great warrior and tactician, but a man of God with faith to be king!"

So the meeting was called with all the elders and other witnesses gathered around David. David's key leaders were with him and they worshiped Yahweh together. David sang some of his songs and played his chordophone. He taught them songs that honored God and called for God to unite and lead the Nation.

Abiathar stepped forward and presented to David a horn filled with oil that elders from the North had brought with them. They prayed and anointed David to be crowned king of all Israel. Although it was a joyous occasion, it was not a party-like atmosphere. It continued into the wee hours of the night, but not in drunken celebration, but rather in praise and worship of Yahweh. It was a time that many present thought could be remembered as a "meeting between heaven and earth." The focus was that everyone knew that God was at the center of this decision. It was God who had "authorized" this man to be their king.

The elders and all there knew in their own hearts this was "from God." They were not simply relying on a prophet to say that God had chosen this man.

While David had waited almost twenty years for this event, he had known for five years that it was going to happen very soon. So he had already planned his first decisions. He and Ahithophel had examined priorities and made clear plans for the first steps of establishing his kingdom. He knew where he was going to establish the capital city. He knew how he would organize his court; he had drawn up plans for his own home. He knew how he would grow the army and the disciplines he would require of his soldiers. He also knew how he would organize and quickly gather his volunteer army from among all the tribes.

All final decisions would now rest in the authority of King David. Whatever he said was law. He could virtually tax the people and require servants to work for him as he alone saw fit. This was the role of a king and David had planned to be the best king and build the strongest nation possible under Yahweh. He would be a benevolent king. He had no perversions of power on his mind. He would care for the poor and the disadvantaged in his kingdom.

David was at the same time a very private person. The only person he allowed into his deepest plans was Ahithophel. Of course he let others talk to him of their ideas but he seldom solicited their thoughts on any matter of state.

He was a very spiritual man and in these last five years he had written many Psalms and had often worshipped the Lord, getting up in the middle of the night to sing to God. David found a life with God that went beyond the life he lived on earth.

This relationship with Yahweh superseded the cares of this world. This world gave him many good things, but it also gave him many problems. He had those who loved him and those who hated him. He had those who would make him king and yet he had lived more than ten years with the king wanting to kill him every day.

The promises of Yahweh did not include a rosy life without its problems. In fact, it seemed to David that the more Yahweh promised, the more difficult life was.

His solution to this dilemma was to worship Yahweh with all his heart and soul and let those things around him be as they may. While in Hebron he had begun to recruit singers and musicians. He started having daily sessions with forty or so singers and forty or so playing musical instruments. They would gather and sing some of David's songs.

One song would flow right into another and there would be a unity in spirit with all present. It was glorious and inspiring to all of the participants to love God and to find how to live for God.

A singer named Asaph became a good friend to the king. David had noticed his deep voice and the sincerity of the man. He came faithfully to every rehearsal David called and was the first one there and the last one to leave.

David engaged him in conversation one day after he had made up his mind to make him the leader of the singers. He said to Asaph, "I found out as a shepherd boy the peace and deep inner confidence that would fill my heart as I sang with all my might unto Yahweh."

David continued, "I am beginning to learn that the experience seems to multiply as more and more of us join together in song and spirit."

Asaph replied, "That is amazing you are talking like this to me. I have been finding this place together in worship a place of unity even in a stronger sense than I feel when I am on the battlefield with my fellow soldiers."

David was excited now, because he knew he found the right man for the job. David jumped in, "Isn't it like experiencing the Presence of Holiness? There is something so cleansing about it. It is as if my deep dark secrets come to light and at the same time washed away. Healing of heart, soul, and body seemed to be in the air."

Asaph excitedly responded, "Oh king truly you are a priest of Yahweh. Your heart is so tender and sensitive to Yahweh, I am so joyful to be chosen by you for such an honored position to lead the singers. I pledge we will be pure in heart first, and hard-working and diligent singers secondly to lead the worship of Yahweh."

David left the room with a humble heart.

From that time forward David began to understand the difference between what took place in the natural realm and what took place in the spiritual realm. David realized that his mind, his will, and his emotions vacillated between these two forces. He had devoted much of his life to developing his spiritual self — the side he wanted to rule his life. But, too often, he found his body or flesh in conflict with his spirit.

David was discovering the common conflicts of man in living this life on earth. On one hand, he sought the Lord with all his mind, will, and emotions. On the other hand, his flesh desired fleshly satisfaction and his mind, will, and emotions seemed to respond to these demands just as easily.

Just as David fought battles on the battlefields he now came to realize he had a major fight within his own soul. He loved Yahweh and expressed that love in worship and benevolence in his rule.

As noble as all this sounds; David had another love growing in his heart as well. He loved being with women and his tastes and indulgences seemed to know no bounds.

CHAPTER TWENTY TWO

U nknown to anyone except Ahithophel, David made his first act as king over Israel the moving of the capital city. He knew the rest of the house of Judah would understand and not be offended — and the location would be of great historical significance. The day after his coronation he declared that Jerusalem would become the capital of the new Israel.

David recalled the words of Moses from Deuteronomy 12: *"But you shall seek the place where the LORD your God chooses, out of all your tribes, to put His name for His dwelling place; and there you shall go. There you shall take your burnt offerings, your sacrifices, your tithes, the heave offerings of your hand, your vowed offerings, your freewill offerings, and the firstborn of your herds and flocks.*

These words were spoken four hundred and sixty three years earlier; Yahweh had told Moses that He would set up a place of "Meeting" with the children of Israel. Prior to David there had been no one who had been able to identify where that place was.

David had already decided how he would build the city of Jerusalem into a jewel for Israel. He devised plans to conscript workers to come to the city monthly. He would provide food and a place to sleep while they worked to build this city of "light.

Ever since David had taken the head of Goliath to Jerusalem so many years before, that city had become a secret obsession in the back of his mind.

It had started with David's reading of scripture. He became fascinated with a king named Melchizedek who was king of Salem. Salem means peace. He was also known in history as the King of righteousness. He was mystical, without a family name, and yet he was real. He evidently had discovered a relationship with God the likes of which no one else had ever found. He learned how to communicate with God in such a fashion that God would interact with him and let Melchizedek know and understand the ways of God —something very few have ever found.

King Melchizedek had met Abraham after Abraham had defeated the conquering kings of the east — those who had pillaged Sodom, Gomorrah, and three other nations eight hundred years before David. They had taken Abraham's nephew Lot and his family, as well as all the spoils.

It had been an unusual time in history because this geographical region had seen much prosperity. On one side there were four kings who banded together to go against five kings, including the kings of Sodom and Gomorrah. The four easily defeated the five. From Sodom came a warrior who had escaped. He had been a friend to Lot and knew of the greatness and blessings upon Abraham.

He came to Abraham and told him of the capture of his nephew. Abraham gathered three hundred and eighteen of his trained servants. Abraham had daily discipline and training of his servants for war. They spent one hour for five days per week strengthening and strategizing and learning to shoot bows and handle swords for fighting against invaders.

Invaders were a common problem in those days and they were near trade routes so possibilities of attack were ever present.

When Abraham received word, within two hours his servants were armed and moving under Abraham's direction. At night they caught up with the celebrating soldiers. Abraham divided his troops into two groups and attacked in the night from both the front and the rear. They caught them sleeping and drunk and with no thought of battle and soundly defeated these five kings even though they had thousands on their side.

They chased down the escapees and gathered all the spoil taken and recovered all the people captured. On their journey home, messengers were sent ahead and the five kings gathered to welcome Abraham. In addition to the five there was another king there to welcome him who was quite mysterious. This king was the king of Salem. His name was Melchizedek. Not only was he a king but he was a priest of "El Yon" – or the "Most High God."

Salem was the old name for what was now called Jerusalem.

As Abraham returned the king of Salem greeted Abraham with "bread and wine." This service was more than to satisfy a hunger from battle, there was a spiritual dimension to the encounter that all felt as if Yahweh was actually present in Person as the nourishment was served.

Then King Melchizedek blessed Abraham with this blessing, "Blessed be Abraham of the Most High God, possessor of heaven and earth. And blessed be El Yon, who has delivered into your hands all your enemies."

Abraham was humbled and knew this was a special moment when God found a way to touch a man on the earth with his Presence. As Abraham bowed he told his servants, "Gather one tenth of all the spoils and give this tenth to this 'king/priest' of the Most High God."

This tithe proved the significance of Melchizedek and his relationship to the Most High God, and it showed the humility and submission of a great man of faith, Abraham.

As David studied this account in scripture, he surmised that Melchizedek walked in a place of authority as a king and yet there was also a place of authority as a priest. David wondered in his own heart if this was a possible place with God for him?

David also took note that when the King of Sodom met Abraham with the other kings present, he had said, "Abraham you have done a great thing. Let all the people return to their homes and you keep all of the bounty."

Abraham responded, "It will not be so. I have lifted my hand in reverence and commitment to the Most High God. I will not lift my hand to another.

"We will keep only what the men needed to sustain them in the battle. I will not even take of a shoe latchet lest any man claim that he made me wealthy. My wealth comes from the Lord."

With David's keen sense of history he knew there was something profoundly spiritual in the kingship of Melchizedek and David sought this identity in his own kingship. He had dreamed in wonder to how the father of his faith, Abraham, had so highly regarded this king priest.

David would consider for the rest of his life how to live out the concept of king/priest — a dual role to be sure. David was also processing what Moses had heard from the Lord as recorded in Exodus chapter 19:

"Then Moses went up to God, and the LORD called to him from the mountain and said, "This is what you are to say to the house of

Jacob and what you are to tell the people of Israel: 'You yourselves have seen what I did to Egypt, and how I carried you on eagles' wings and brought you to myself. Now if you obey me fully and keep my covenant, then out of all nations you will be my treasured possession. Although the whole earth is mine, you will be for me a kingdom of priests and a holy nation.' These are the words you are to speak to the Israelites."

David was seeking to understand how to implement and integrate the spiritual man, a man who walked with God and understood the ways of God, and yet was a man who lived and worked on the earth.

These nearly twenty years of waiting for this day of coronation, and especially the last five years, manifesting the promises and purposes of God, found David pondering the significance of the moment. All he could dream about was how this fit into history. He saw man as an extension of God on earth. He saw God who chose to limit himself on earth until He could find men that would agree with him and perform or live out his will on earth. As David read the Bible he saw that this mysterious King Melchizedek must have been such a man.

David knew much about God as he learned to worship and at the same time listen to his own heart being opened to the influence he felt was from God. David knew that every high priest is selected from among men and is appointed to represent them in matters related to God, to offer gifts and sacrifices for sins. The priest is able to deal gently with those who are ignorant and are going astray, since he himself is subject to weakness. This is why he has to offer sacrifices for his own sins, as well as for the sins of the people. No one takes this honor upon himself; he must be called by God, just as Aaron was.

David was also captured by the limited explanation in the Word of God about this "king/priest" Melchizedek. As he was dreaming one day about this man he wrote a song about him: (Psalm 110)

The LORD said to my Lord, "Sit in honor at my right hand until I humble your enemies, making them a footstool under your feet."

The LORD will extend your powerful dominion from Jerusalem, you will rule over your enemies.

In that day of battle, your people will serve you willingly. Arrayed in holy garments, your vigor will be renewed each day like the morning dew.

The LORD has taken an oath and will not break his vow: "You are a priest forever in the line of Melchizedek."

The Lord stands at your right hand to protect you. He will strike down many kings in the day of his anger.

He will punish the nations and fill them with their dead; he will shatter heads over the whole earth. But he himself will be refreshed from brooks along the way. He will be victorious.

For the first time in all of his meditations, David began to connect with the future as well as the past. He was beginning to realize that being made king was not the end of the will of God but only the beginning. He was realizing that not only was he to build a powerful kingdom, but that kingdom was to be to the glory of God.

That God would use the nation of Israel to proclaim to the world God's greatness and to proclaim his glory.

David, based on his connection with the past started the move to Jerusalem the day after his coronation. For after all, David had been planning the move for at least seven years and six months.

But all the rest of his planning was with a view to the future and his dreams for the greatest kingdom on earth. He was beginning to sense that Yahweh was revealing an eternal dimension to the concept of king/priest.

He sought to discover more.

CHAPTER TWENTY THREE

D avid took all of his troops to lead the people with him to Jerusalem. The inhabitants of Jerusalem at that time were a people called the Jebusites. When Joshua conquered Israel he had not bothered the Jebusites because they were not a warlike people. A high percentage of the population was inbred and many were lame and blind.

David's troops marched in discipline and order, not to enter into war but to lead a procession of all of his key followers and those who were going to live with him in his city.

David did not intend to kill the Jebusites so he sent a handful of soldiers to order them to leave the city.

But the elders of the Jebusites had a curious reply. Thinking David would be too proud to fight such people, they answered, "You cannot come here or we will send the lame and the blind to fight you."

But they misunderstood his resolve. David asked for volunteers to get rid of the Jebusites. David offered a reward, "Whoever goes up to the Jebusites and clears them out of there, I will make him a captain."

It was quick work and David vanquished the city the next day with most of the Jebusites gone. He took a corner of the city as his home and headquarters. This corner was called Zion or Mount Zion. It was about a twenty acre site and David called this portion the "City of David." This portion was uneven land on a hill. David had the site backfilled and leveled out. The site was near the spring later called Gihon that provided water to the entire city for millennia.

It gave him a commanding view of all approaches to the city from the east and overlooked the valley later called Kidron. It also looked over a place later called the Mount of Olives. David and the people prospered here. David was excited; his dreams were becoming his reality. He was up early, praying and then energizing his workers to rebuild the city according to his vision.

On the coast near Israel was Tyre, a land with wonderful forests of cedar trees. Its king was Hiram, a Phoenician, and he welcomed the kingship of David and sent hundreds of cedar trees with carpenters and masons in order to build David a house fit for a king.

This confirmed in David's heart that the Lord had established David as king and that He was exalting his kingdom over all the earth as a testimony to all the children of Israel. David was always alert to what God was showing him by working through others. When a former enemy built a magnificent house for him he knew that God was moving the hearts of people.

David seemed invincible. He was a mighty warrior with no peer. He was a great leader that all would follow. He was a "man of God" who loved and praised his Lord.

But David did have a glaring weakness. His penchant for women had been a growing issue in his life. And now, he would take the time to indulge his sexual dreams with more women in his life. He already had six wives by the time he came to Jerusalem. He had two wives when he first got to Hebron and added four while there. But in Jerusalem he acquired additional wives and eleven more children added to the six he already had. He also took concubines, women that were his and available to him without being married. It was becoming a full time job for Hushai to keep scouting for the available beauties of Israel.

This weakness brought confusion within his house. Women vied for preeminence and many tried to promote their children for special recognition by David whenever they could.

One of the dynamic relationships was with his first wife, Michal. She had been the love of his life as his first woman. She was more beautiful with age. They had been teenagers when her father Saul had given her to him. They had been magically in love and could not keep their hands from each other every moment they were together.

In Michal's love for David she protected him against the threat of her father to kill him. She proved her loyalty but the years of separation when David was avoiding Saul took their toll. Her father had given her to another man who was also a loving husband, a man who made her the center of his world. Michal knew that with David as king with many other wives her time as center of his attention was long past.

There was no doubt in the household who was in charge – it was clearly David. He was a strong leader and decisive and a man with much to do. But constant pressure from the women in his life did wear on him and sometimes affected his thinking.

David set rules with the women. They were never allowed to walk into any room he was in. He refused to look over his shoulder wondering who was watching. So his women had to request an appointment or a time with him. Of course, they also had to be available to him at a moment's notice.

The woman's role was secondary and submissive throughout the society to be sure. Oddly though, the mother's role was one of great power and influence in the society. Many times the lineage was traced through the mother's side of the family. Likewise, many times it was the mother who pushed or manipulated the sons to action or position.

Although David's mother had virtually no influence over him, his wives, as mothers, were constantly behind the scenes positioning their sons in the line of succession.

David had a heart for Yahweh but he also had a heart for any beautiful woman.

CHAPTER TWENTY FOUR

David grew in strength and might. His army was stronger than ever – he had his thirty thousand full time, highly trained and totally committed troops. And more soldiers desired to join daily.

The Philistines no longer had their way taxing the tribes at will. David also had a solid volunteer army training program and was acquiring weapons for both the regular army and the volunteers.

He had men who could accurately fire a bow from 200 yards for a kill. He had men who could kill tens of the enemies in a day and some could kill hundreds. He had men who could kill in hand-to-hand combat, kill with pointed goads, kill with the sword, and there was no match among the enemy to the training David had started many years ago back at the cave of Adullan.

The Philistines wanted to launch an all-out attack on David early in his reign. They were hoping to catch him before he could properly organize his army. They certainly knew he was very capable so they gathered their army and came for David quickly after his coronation. They marched to the valley at Rephaim and deployed themselves.

David asked the Lord, "Should I go up against the Philistines, and will you deliver them into my hands?"

The Lord answered, "Go up and I will doubtless give them into your hands." The word "doubtless" was an important word to David. This word from God charged his faith with authority and all doubt was extinguished in his heart and mind.

David gathered his fulltime troops and went up to a place he later called Baal Perazim to wage war. The Philistines took images of all their gods with them. They knew how spiritual David was and how he gloated over the fact that "his God" gave him victory every time. So they decided to call upon their own gods to wage this war.

David defeated them soundly at Baal Perazim and chased them on the run. They ran without taking any of their gods with them. David and his men took those idols and marched after the Philistines.

They retreated to the Valley of Rephaim again. David paused and asked the Lord, "Should I go up after them again?"

The Lord said, "You shall not go up against them head on. Rather go around behind them but in front of the forest of mulberry trees that are there. Then wait for the 'sound of marching' in the tops of the mulberry trees. When you hear that sound go quickly for then the Lord will go before you to strike the camp of the Philistines."

David got his men into position. He stood proud and tall with his sword raised high. His men looked to him for the signal. Even though they were completely outnumbered there was faith in the camp. They all believed in David and David believed in the direction and power of Yahweh.

David listened, and then suddenly the sound came in the tops of the trees and David and his men went forth in faith believing that God was going before them. The Philistines interpreted the wind blowing in the trees as the sound of the enemy marching against them and attacking them from the rear with more troops coming from the front. In the confusion the Philistines panicked and ran in two different directions.

David and his men drove the Philistines from Geba to Gazer, killing them every step of the way.

David declared that day, "The Lord has broken through my enemies before me, like a breakthrough of water"

This became a principle of understanding between God and his people under the direction of David. Unexplainable events would take place in the camp of the enemies. They would fall under confusion and the camp would be filled with chaos. Orders would not be understood, or they would turn on each other without understanding what they were doing.

This became a pattern when the armies of Israel would go forth in the name of the Most High God. Regardless of the odds, they could achieve victory as they fought in faith, submitting to Yahweh and trusting him for every step.

And the fame of David went out into all lands; and the Lord brought the fear of him upon all nations. David began to realize other nations were responding to his army's assaults with strange reactions. He thought it quite irrational that opposing armies would fall into such confusion even to the place of killing each other. His conclusion was surly Yahweh was somehow clouding the thoughts of his enemies.

CHAPTER TWENTY FIVE

D avid, the dreamer, had become a ruler and implementer of his dreams. His years in Hebron ruling over Judah did not tax his time and talent. He had plenty of time to draw up his plans. He designed his priorities and established his action steps when he became king over all Israel. He had absolute confidence that it would happen. He had dreamed about what the kingdom would look like to outsiders. He thought of his palace, and even more than that, he dreamed of building a temple as a House for the Lord. He wanted it to be like no other building on earth.

To make all of that happen, not only would he need much gold and silver, but he would need laborers. He commanded twenty four thousand workers per month assigned proportionally from among the tribes. These twenty four thousand were led by a captain from each tribe and were broken down into thousands, hundreds, and fifties with captains over each to serve the king in the capital. David himself organized these work crews and gave them their work assignments.

There is no way to explain David's understandings of building and design. David knew it was inspiration of the Holy Spirit. Ever since he had been anointed to be king as a teenager and he was filled with the Holy Spirit, he found in prayer that he could tap into knowledge from Yahweh through the Holy Spirit. In prayer and worship he could see how to backfill land, how to build foundations for buildings, and how to design and build the buildings themselves.

It was miraculous to see this warrior king have such brilliant understanding, not only how to build and design a city and buildings, but how to pull together a nation united with a disciplined army.

David put together all aspects of life to be centered on accomplishing the will of God for daily living.

David organized worship life in Jerusalem. He made sure that the priesthood was pure and from the house of Aaron, the lineage chosen under Moses to manage feasts times and weekly worship. He developed services requiring four thousand musicians to play along with dancers and singers.

David assigned Asaph and his sons to lead and teach the playing with harps, cymbals, and an instrument called a psaltery. A psaltery was a type of harp. It had twelve strings and was usually played sitting on someone's lap, although it could be played while one walked.

David, after all of his years of playing instruments, learned and taught others how to "prophesy" with their instruments. It was done by playing a melody and thinking about and worshipping the Lord. As they played, the sounds that came forth would seem as if the Lord inspired the musician making music to play music never heard before. A song would come forth for the first time and words would often come to the heart of the player or those standing near and they would begin singing and creating a brand new song.

David, with the help of Asaph, developed the choir for the capital. He had two hundred and eighty-eight singers who worked at song fulltime. They trained daily, developing their voices, creating songs, working as one large choir and various smaller groups depending upon the music and forum they would play in for the king but always unto the Lord. They also lived life in purity keeping their daily lives accountable to Asaph.

The Levites, as they were called, came from the house of Levi, one of the twelve tribes of Israel. They also performed the sacrificial burnt offerings required under the Mosaic Law. David made worship services not just a religious exercise for the priesthood. He went so far as to have services twice a day, in the morning and at evening time.

He involved the people throughout the city and each service was a production unto itself. Thousands of participants enabling tens of thousands to become involved as they all worshipped the Lord.

The meetings would begin from the palace as the musicians marched out blowing the shofars and calling the people to order and attention. Next came forth the chordophones, tambourines, cymbals, lyres and drums giving the beat and rhythm for the singers who came next.

The musicians were arrayed in a semi-circle with the singers in front of them. Then the dancers came with banners and flags twirling and the sound filled the city. There was nothing sensual about it. It was all directed to the Most High God. Yahweh was in everyone's thoughts and hearts as they sang, played, and danced.

Periodically, there would be the call for the sacrifice of animals. These times brought a drama that was led by the Levites who were appointed to all service of the tabernacle of the house of God. Aaron and his sons who were over the age of twenty, offered upon the altar of the burnt offering, and on the altar of incense and were appointed for all the work of the place most holy, and to make atonement for Israel, according to all that Moses the servant of God had commanded.

The Levites would bring in an ox for example. It would be led in after the singing and music had been playing for as much as an hour. The animal would be led to the altar and there his throat would be slashed.

The participants would continue in song without stopping. The priests would hold the animal as it bled out, with blood flowing over the altar area. On some occasions there would be more than one animal sacrificed.

The blood and death of the animal would be done unto the Lord. The sacrifice was first an expense. It cost the animal's owner money. Secondly, the blood sacrifice was an example of the payment necessary for the sins of the people. Payment of sins by blood is required by Yahweh. This was the economy that Yahweh decreed from the Creation.

Man was born in perfection, but the power to choose was given to man so that he could live or not live under the authority of Yahweh. Man chose to sin against Yahweh so then Yahweh decreed that the only answer for sin was the shedding of blood.

During the time of Moses and continuing into the time of David, the sacrifice of animals represented a picture of the sacrifice that Yahweh planned as the solution to resolve the sins of man. At the time of David, they knew that Yahweh would one day provide the ultimate sacrifice that would be acceptable as payment for the sins of man – but they could not quite see what that meant.

In addition to the singers and priests assigned to duties, David assigned Shelomith and his brethren over all the treasures of those things dedicated to the Lord. This included all manner of gold and silver items which could be melted down and made into the utensils needed for the House of the Lord.

Out of the house of Korah came the porters and the gatekeepers for the city. David left nothing to chance. There was organization to all phases of life from the military to the spiritual life of the people and down to the coming and going in and out of the city by all the population and visitors.

Quite carefully, David made sure he was not in the center of any of the worship experiences he established for the people. The last thing he wanted was to get anyone's attention off of Yahweh and onto him. He participated joyfully in every service, but was out of the limelight and could not be seen by many.

CHAPTER TWENTY SIX

As the worship services started taking over the spiritual attention of the people, David thought it was now time to recover what was called the Ark of the Lord (sometimes called the Ark of the Covenant)and bring it to Jerusalem. While they had always been forbidden to make with their hands any physical representation of God, the Ark was not that.

In keeping with his felt mandate to combine the spiritual side of life with daily life in this world, David thought it fitting for the Ark to come to Jerusalem. He believed it was God's will that it should be placed in the Tabernacle, which had been built by Moses, which now was being called the "Tabernacle of David."

David consulted widely with the people to secure their approval and support to bring the Ark to Jerusalem. He was challenging the people that God had not been sought through the Ark the whole time that Saul ruled. The people, in one accord, agreed to support the effort and to participate in honoring God in this way.

Just as he dreamed and sought to understand how Melchizedek functioned as a king/priest combination, so he desired to live out that combination. And restoring the Ark of the Lord to prominence was a step in that direction.

The Ark of the Lord was an ornamental chest that contained special items that reminded all of Israel of the historic interventions by God with his people at a critical time in their history. The chest was a little over three cubits long and one cubit and a hand breadth wide and the same high. It was made of acacia wood overlaid with pure gold both inside and outside. There were four legs with feet to the chest and a gold ring on the outside of each leg. A pole of acacia wood would go through the rings and that was how the Ark was to be carried.

In addition, there were two cherubim made out of hammered gold. They had wings spread out and they overshadowed the chest. There was also a seat built of acacia wood and also overlaid with gold and placed on the top of the Ark and between the Cherubim – it was called the Mercy Seat.

Inside the Ark was placed: manna, which had been their food in the wilderness for forty years, two tablets on which were written the Ten Commandments, the rod of Aaron that budded even though the staff was not alive, and a part of a tree that testified that Aaron and his descendants were to be the priests of God.

This represented the "Presence of God" to the people of Israel. The Ark had been housed at a village named Shiloh under Samuel. When the Philistines conquered Shiloh, killing thirty thousand soldiers of Israel, they captured the Ark and took it with them back to their city.

As news came to the priest Eli, who had raised Samuel, that the Ark had been taken he fell over with a heart attack. His daughter in law was at the moment of giving birth and she died in childbirth. The baby boy was born and they named him Ichabod, and this name had a meaning, "the glory has departed" from his people.

The Philistines brought the Ark to Ashdod, the city of their god named Dagon. They put the Ark into the same room where a statue of Dagon stood. The next morning they found Dagon's statue lying on its face. They stood it up and left them together again. The next day they walked in and the head of Dagon and both of his hands were cut off and lying on the threshold.

The mystery here is that no person had entered the temple during either night. There was no natural explanation for the events of Dagon's head and hands being cut off or for that matter for Dagon falling over and lying down in the Presence of the Ark of God.

The Philistines were in a quandary. The priests of Dagon never again came into the house of Dagon. In addition, plagues broke out upon the people with all kinds of sickness and disease. These people were aware of the power of gods and of course had been under the delusion that their god was greater. But the events taking place were forcing them to acknowledge that Yahweh was the Great God. Rather than attempting to convert to the ways of Yahweh, they merely tried to figure out how to pacify him.

They sent the Ark to the city of Gath. The hand of the Lord came against this city as well as all the men of the city got severe bowel problems and were sick and dying. They then took the Ark to Ekron, another city of the Philistines. Great destruction came to the city as it had to the other cities. Thousands died and others had tumors and hemorrhoids.

They gathered their priests serving all of their gods and asked what should they do? The priests advised sending the Ark back with an offering to appease the Most High God. They put the Ark on a cart and said let the oxen take the Ark where they were led.

The Ark went to Bethshemesh and the men there looked into the Ark to see all that was there. A wave of destruction came to those men and the Lord destroyed fifty thousand and seventy men in one day. It was forbidden for just anyone to look in there. One had to be in right relationship with Yahweh. That relationship meant only from someone among the priesthood who understood and followed the rules of preparation and the lifestyle required.

Word came to the men of Kirjathjearim in Israel that the Ark had returned from the Philistines, so they retrieved the Ark and housed it at the home of Abinadab and set aside his son, Eleazar to keep and watch over the Ark.

The Ark rested there for over twenty years until David now went to retrieve it to bring it to the city that David believed God wanted to be the capital of the kingdom of Israel.

Growing in the mind of David was the idea that there was a potential merging of the kingdom of Israel and the Kingdom of God on earth. David felt that God had always intended to reveal who He is to the whole earth. Now that David had ascended to the throne, he began to dream how he could help make that happen.

He was certainly conflicted over this "merging" concept. The problem he readily saw was that Yahweh was Holy and Righteous and Pure. At the same time mankind was not any of those things. Yet he felt God wanted a merger and he knew that only God could figure out how this could be possible.

David wanted the recovery of the Ark to be the biggest spiritual demonstration and the most dramatic event ever seen in the world. He wanted to organize it down to the smallest details so that all who would witness the event would dramatize the stories down through the coming ages.

He again gathered thirty thousand of his fulltime army. They were organized into three main bodies and marched in order. He delegated harpists, flutists, and singers to lead the procession. There were those with timbrels and cymbals and wind instruments playing together in harmony and joy unto the Lord.

All were joyful in this wonderful day of celebration when the cart carrying the Ark was going through Gibeah, the former capital city. The cart started tilting as if to fall. One of David's men named Uzzah, leaped to the cart to hold it to make sure it did not fall over. Suddenly, the Lord was angry at Uzzah for touching the Ark and struck him dead.

A hush instantly came over the entire procession. David was shocked, sad, and angry at the same time. Everything stopped and David stood in wonder trying to decide what to do next.

David told his men, "Take the cart and lead the oxen over to the house of Obededom the Gittite. Let him care for it until I determine what the Lord would have me to do."

Three months later David was told that the house of Obededom had suddenly prospered to overflowing for the past three months. David took that as a sign that God wanted him to proceed with the Ark to bring it to Jerusalem, but to make sure that no one touched it on the cart.

David gathered together all the troops and musicians and singers and started the procession up again to bring the Ark up to the City of David.

So the priests and the Levites sanctified themselves with washings and fasting, to bring up the Ark of the Lord God of Israel. The children of the Levites carried the Ark of God upon their shoulders with the staves thereon, as Moses commanded according to the word of the Lord.

David spoke to the chief of the Levites to appoint their brethren to be the singers with instruments of music, psalteries and harps and cymbals, sounding, by lifting up their voices with joy. Every six steps David had a sacrifice of oxen or fatling. The worship gained momentum especially at each sacrifice. All knew that something special was in this procession. They all had a sense once again of the Presence of Yahweh. Joy and awe filled every heart.

And David was clothed with a robe of fine linen, and all the Levites that bare the ark, and the singers, and Chenaniah the master of the song with the singers: David also was wearing an ephod of linen. The worship took on a particular frenzy the closer they got to the Tabernacle David had prepared.

David began tearing off his robe and began to dance leading the procession. He danced without restraint, this great warrior, leader and king stripped off his clothes leaving on only a small linen wrap around his waist. He was acting as if he had lost his mind; his eyes glazed over and sweat pouring over his body. He danced with all his might and sang with all his heart.

All the people gathered along the way and they all got caught up in the moment with singing and shouting to be heard for miles. The trumpets ushered every step with sounds of the majesty of heaven and all were caught up in the heaven on earth feeling of wonder and amazement.

They were bringing the Ark into the tabernacle that David had prepared. As they got closer coming up the hill to the City of David, or Mount Zion, they got closer to his home. His wife Michal, Saul's daughter, looked upon David with shame and disgust and despised him in her heart.

As they brought the Ark into the Tabernacle David began making peace offerings and burnt offerings unto the Lord. When the Ark was settled down, David blessed the people in the Name of the Lord, similar to the manner of a priest. He then brought out food and wine for all the thousands of people who had participated in the worship of Yahweh.

Then David returned to bless his own household and all his wives and children and concubines and servants. Michal jumped out front to stop him with anger showing in her flushed red face.

"How glorious the king of Israel was today, who uncovered himself in the eyes of the handmaids of his servants, as one of the party goers would do among the young men."

There is something that rises up in the hearts of people during the worship of the Lord. True worship, the kind that is sincere and heartfelt, stirs humility and awe in the hearts of believers. But in the hearts of unbelievers when they witness true worship it stirs anger and resentment over the display. Michal's response revealed her unbelief.

David retorted, "It was the Lord who chose me before your father, and before his entire house to appoint me ruler over the people of the Lord, over Israel. Therefore I will play before the Lord and I will be even viler than what you saw today."

He continued, "I will be base in mine own eyes, and these poor maidservants you talk about, of them I shall be in more honor."

The division between them was irreconcilable. Michal the daughter of Saul was withheld from ever having a child unto the day of her death. God's approval of David was clear and nothing was to diminish the joy and significance of the Ark of God located in the City of David. It was noted by friend and foe that blessings came as the Ark resided in the prepared Tabernacle giving honor and glory to the Most High God built by David. David wrote:

He is the LORD our God; his judgments are in all the earth.

> **He remembers his covenant forever, the word He commanded, for a thousand generations, the covenant he made with Abraham, the oath He swore to Isaac.**

> **He confirmed it to Jacob as a decree to Israel as an everlasting covenant: "To you I will give the land of Canaan as the portion you will inherit."**

> **When they were but few in number, few indeed, and strangers in it, they wandered from nation to nation, from one kingdom to another.**

He allowed no man to oppress them; for their sake he rebuked kings: Do not touch my anointed ones; do my prophets no harm. Sing to the LORD, all the earth; proclaim his salvation day after day.

Declare his glory among the nations, his marvelous deeds among all peoples. For great is the LORD and most worthy of praise; He is to be feared above all gods. For all the gods of the nations are idols, but the LORD made the heavens.

> David was realizing and declaring that Yahweh had chosen to obligate himself to be the God of Israel as an example to the world. God had promised them land that was not totally under their control. He chose them when they were small in number as to prove it was not who they were or what they had accomplished as being the reason why He chose them.

But David saw the need for the people to sing unto the Lord and proclaim his salvation. This worship would give the people a sense of Yahweh and enable Yahweh to communicate to the people through the worship.

David began holding two regular worship services per day around the Tabernacle now that the Ark was where it belonged. Thousands and thousands gathered and participated.

CHAPTER TWENTY SEVEN

Things went well for David. His enemies were quiet for the time being. David had discovered a man named Nathan who was a prophet of God. Nathan became his closest spiritual advisor. While Ahithophel only wanted to talk about matters of state, David could talk with Nathan as someone who understood life from both the spiritual dimension and the political point of view as well.

One day David said to Nathan, "I dwell in this wonderful house built out of cedar and the Ark of God dwells in a place made by Moses with curtains as the walls. It doesn't seem right to me."

"While this Tabernacle was built after a pattern shown by God to Moses, today it seems inadequate. We are a people no longer on the move and now it only seems right that we would build something to be more representative of the Glory due unto Yahweh."

Nathan agreed with the logic and responded, "Do what is in your heart, for the Lord is certainly with you."

But that night the word of the Lord came to Nathan saying, *"Go tell my servant David, thus says the Lord, you shall not build me a house for me to dwell in. I have not dwelt in a house since the time that I brought up the children of Israel out of Egypt four hundred and sixty three years ago.*

"But I have walked in a tent and in a tabernacle until this day. Have I at any time asked anyone to build me a house of cedar?

"So tell my servant David, Thus says the Lord of hosts, I took you from shepherding a few sheep to be ruler over my people, over Israel.

"I was with you wherever you went. I have cut off all your enemies and have made you a great name like unto the great men that have ever been on the earth.

"Moreover, I will appoint a place for my people Israel and will plant them that they may dwell in a place of their own and move no more, neither shall the children of wickedness afflict them anymore.

"And as your days are fulfilled and you shall sleep with your fathers, I will set up your seed after you that come out of your own loins and I will establish his kingdom.

"He shall build a house for my name and I will establish the throne of his kingdom forever. I will be his Father and he will be my son. If he commits sin I will chasten him with the rod of men.

"But my mercy shall not depart away from him like it did with Saul. Your house and your kingdom shall be established forever before you. Your throne shall be established forever!"

Nathan repeated all of these words to David the next morning. The promises of God were overwhelming to David. He was at once humbled and awestruck at how personal Yahweh was with him.

David wondered out loud to Nathan, "This is beyond any dream I have ever had. The Lord promising me to be a king of a kingdom that will last forever! How could it be possible that all that come from my loins in all succeeding generations could live up to the standards of Yahweh?"

David went into the Tabernacle and sat before the Lord and began to talk out loud, *"Who am I O Lord God? And what is my family that you have brought me to such a time and place.*

"I know this is a small thing in your sight, O Lord God, but you have spoken of my house with a future that is hard to grasp for a man.

"What can I say to you Lord? You know me and my limitations. For your word's sake and according to your own heart you have done all of these great things and have allowed me to know them and understand them.

"You are a great God, O Lord God; there is none like you and there is no other God beside you that any of us have ever heard of.

"What one nation in the earth is like your people Israel, whom God went to redeem for a people to himself and to make him a name, and to do great things for your land and before your people which you redeemed from Egypt and from the gods of Egypt?

"You are confirming today that the people of Israel are a people to you forever and you are their God.

"And now, O Lord God, the word you have spoken concerning me and my house, establish it forever and do as you have said!

"Let your name be magnified forever and let the Lord of hosts be God over Israel, and let the house of your servant David be established before you.

"For you, O Lord of hosts, God of Israel, has revealed to your servant that you will build yourself a house and I accept that. And now O Lord God, you are God, and your words are true and you have promised goodness to me your servant.

"Let it please you to bless the house of your servant that it may continue forever before you. You have spoken it and with your blessing let the house of your servant be blessed forever."

David could barely walk out of the tabernacle. He was drained of all emotions as he considered the meaning and the ramifications of all the spoken words that day between God and him.

These words from the Most High God and David's expressed understanding of these words brought a new dimension to David's relationship with Nathan. It was no longer David showing honor only to those men of faith who had come before him like Abraham and Moses connecting him with the past now there was a certain future that needed to be included and considered in every decision.

With promises from God that included a word like "forever" David continued to think about life on earth from a whole different perspective. In his heart he began to consider eternity. His view of life previously had been oriented to connecting to the past. Now he began to grasp the future and the ramifications of future effects on present decisions.

Furthermore, he began to see the transcendence of God over the temporary actions and shortfalls of men on this earth. An eternal perspective diminished the pain and pressures of life on earth. Everything in the moment became a little less serious.

God was declaring and identifying a relationship with people that went to another realm beyond life as it is known on this earth. It now became clear to David that it was God's will to establish the Kingdom of God using the children of Israel as his starting point.

It was mind-numbing to think about his throne – David's throne – as a symbolic one, which would be filled forever! David had difficulty comprehending that a mortal man could fulfill such a promise. The idea of "forever" went beyond even the dreams of this lifelong dreamer.

There were no easy understandings of these thoughts. They would need to percolate in his heart and mind and it could take a lifetime to grasp them — if at all.

But one thing David did know. As God had been with the children of Israel, starting with Abraham, and into and out of Egypt under the leadership of Moses, likewise God was with David and the children of Israel here in the Land of Promise.

CHAPTER TWENTY EIGHT

As time went on, David continued his defeat of the Philistines and took over a city they controlled called Metheg Ammah. He also defeated the Moabites extending his kingdom further to the east.

He chose not to annihilate all of the Moabites for there had been some family connection in ages past. He made them line up and measured them off in groups of three. He had the first two killed and the third was allowed to live. From then on the remaining third was to bring tribute to David for allowing them to live.

David continued his campaign and fought the king of Zobah to gain control all along the Euphrates. He captured one thousand chariots, seven thousand charioteers, and twenty thousand foot soldiers. He disabled all but one hundred of the chariot horses, picking out the best for his army.

In battle David was a fearsome warrior. He had ten armor bearers with him at all times. They were not just to protect him but were there to assist him. He always had Goliath's sword carried by one of them. When the right rage came over him he would call for the "sword of the giant." They would hand it to him and he would start swinging it killing everyone he hit.

David killed tens of men in these battles. The power and success of the warfare in his armies was unheard of in the world at that time.

Such power extended to others with David. In one battle, Abishai killed three hundred of the enemy with his spear alone. The extraordinary strength required for such exploits could only come from the Holy Spirit.

Benaiah was another valiant man. He slew two lion-like men from Moab. He went down into a pit and slew a lion. An Egyptian attacked him with a spear and he took the spear away from him and killed him with his own spear.

Adino killed an astounding 800 men in one day's battle with his spear. Eleazar was another mighty man who killed so many of the enemy in one day that his sword could not be removed from his hand as he went to sleep that night, because it had become an extension of his arm.

Another mighty man, Shammah, had a field of lentils and the Philistines gathered troops to steal his harvest. He stood in the field and said to them, "This is my field and my harvest, and no one shall touch it!" He stood alone as everyone with him fled at the sight of the troops. But Shammah killed them all and every one of them.

At that time the Arameans of Damascus came to help the king of Zobah. David took them on as well striking down twenty-two thousand. He then created a base of operations with a garrison of soldiers in Damascus.

The Lord gave David victory wherever he went!

The Most High God, or Yahweh, was a jealous God. He, as the Creator, would not tolerate the worship of other gods. As Yahweh had proven over and over again, these false gods could not stand before him or his chosen people. The people of Israel had been chosen to represent Yahweh so that others might learn to worship the True and Living God.

The Most High God gave others a chance to turn to him. But in their refusal they became subject to judgment here on earth. David and his army became the instrument of that judgment.

The king of Zobah was named Hadadezer and he had a wealthy kingdom. His soldiers had gold shields which David's men gathered and brought to Jerusalem. David also took large quantities of bronze from all the cities of Hadadezer.

Tou, king of Hamath was previously an enemy of Hadadezer and when he heard of David's victories he prudently sent his son Joram to bring gifts of silver and gold and bronze in congratulations. King David dedicated these articles to the Lord as he had done with all the gold and silver he had won from all of his enemies.

Returning to Jerusalem, David encountered the Edomites near the Valley of Salt at the Dead Sea is. It is called the Dead Sea because the concentration of salt is so high that nothing can live in those waters. It is also over twelve hundred and fifty feet below sea level.

David conquered the Edomites killing eighteen thousand soldiers. He left garrisons of soldiers to watch over his new interests there as the Edomites became subject to David, as had all of the other vanquished enemies.

The Lord continued to give David victory wherever he went.

With such rapid expansion, David began delegating responsibility to more of his faithful men. He built outposts wherever he gained victory to secure the territory so they would not have to re-conquer it in the future.

The strategy was to defeat a city or region and leave an occupying force with control of the politics and the economy. This was a new strategy in this region of the world and in this time in history.

In spite of the previous glaring transgression by Joab, David put him in charge of all armed forces. He was given the responsibility to name leaders under him, to establish communications and order with all foreign garrisons, and to expand training programs for both full time and volunteer soldiers. Key leaders still needed David's approval, but this showed that David was quite secure in his own position to trust a man like Joab with such extended responsibilities.

It was during this time that David established his "Top Thirty," of the most proven and faithful warriors. All of them had been with him since the cave of Adullan and had risen to the top ranks through courage displayed and their faithfulness to obey every command.

 King David selected Jehoshaphat as his secretary to track all decisions, appointments, all battles, and all tribute due from conquering lands. David kept precise counts of those killed and wounded in every battle. He tracked the bounty and riches that was won and due the victor.

He selected Zadok and Ahimelech as chief priests. David was careful to make sure there was oversight to the religious life of his people. They were to monitor local priests, run the national feasts that took place three times per year, and make sure the spiritual life was properly cultivated and a part of daily living throughout the nation.

The last thing King David wanted was all the "spiritual power" residing in one man. He thought it best to have two men to keep this spiritual influence diffused so he would not have to struggle with another Samuel as Saul had to do. At the same time he named a secretary to record the progress and working of God in the nation, and his name was Saraiah. He named Benaiah to give oversight to the Kerethites and Pelethites, who were conquered people. David's sons were named royal advisors and given access to him. He regularly shared his major decisions with them.

As order was established throughout the kingdom, King David began to think about Jonathan, his best friend in life. If only Jonathan could have survived to be with David at this time? After all he was the one who convinced David that the prophecy would come true and that David was certainly to be the king.

One day David asked his advisors, "Is there anyone still left of the house of Saul to whom I can show kindness for Jonathan's sake?" They knew of a servant that was in Saul's house named Ziba and they called him to appear before the king.

The king said to him, "Are you Ziba?"

"I am your servant," he replied.

The king asked, "Is there not anyone still left of the house of Saul to whom I can show God's kindness?"

Ziba answered, "There is still a son of Jonathan; he is crippled in both feet."

"Where is he?" the king asked.

Ziba answered, "He is at the house of Makir, son of Ammiel in Lo Debar."

Ironically, Lo Debar was a place of dumping refuse of Jerusalem. Mephibosheth was hiding there as his natural expectation was he could die by the king's hand for being a possible successor to the throne. He had heard of David's promise to his father, but cautiously thought it was better to keep quiet.

In his own mind he also had a claim on the throne should something happen to David, so all the more reason to stay behind the scenes.

King David was excited because now he could fulfill his last promise to his best friend in life. He could extend protection and kindness to an heir of Jonathan. So he sent for him to be brought to the palace.

This son's name was Mephibosheth and he was brought before the king, bowing in his presence.

David said, "Mephibosheth!"

"Your servant my lord," he replied

"Don't be afraid," David assured him, "for I will surely show you kindness for the sake of your father Jonathan. I will restore to you all the land that belonged to your grandfather Saul and you will always eat at my table!"

Mephibosheth bowed lower still and said, "What is your servant that you should notice a dead dog like me?"

The king summoned Ziba and said to him, "I have given your master's grandson everything that belonged to Saul and his family. You and your sons and servants are to farm the land for him and bring in the crops, so that your master's grandson may be provided for. And Mephibosheth, grandson of your master, will always eat at my table."

Ziba had fifteen sons and twenty servants, so they were of the means to manage such holdings that David was bestowing on Mephibosheth.

Then Ziba said to the king, "Your servant will do whatever my lord the king commands his servant to do."

So Mephibosheth ate at David's table like one of the king's sons. Mephibosheth had a young son named Mica and Mephibosheth lived in Jerusalem with his wife and son and ate daily at the king's table, and he was all his life crippled in both feet.

CHAPTER TWENTY NINE

Most people who observed David and heard of his exploits, or who were survivors of his victories often misunderstood him and his decision making. On one hand he was brutal and decisive, leaving no prisoners at times, and on the other hand, showing mercy and blessings even to his enemies.

In the course of time, the king of the Ammonites died and his son Hanun succeeded him as king. David, when he heard the news, thought, "I will show kindness to Hanun son of Nahash, just as his father showed kindness to me."

So David sent a delegation to express his sympathy to Hanun concerning his father. When David's men came to the land of the Ammonites, the Ammonite nobles said to Hanun their new king, "Do you think David is honoring your father by sending men to you to express sympathy?

"Hasn't King David sent them to you to explore the city and spy it out so that he can more easily overthrow it?"

So Hanun made a fateful decision. Rather than verify their motives first, he assumed to make a display of power by saying, "I will show you that you can't come into my city under the guise of sympathy!"

Hanun seized David's men, and shamed them in a degrading fashion by shaving off half of each man's beard; he had them cut off their garments in the middle of the buttocks, and sent them away.

When it was reported to King David, he told the men, "stay at Jericho until your beards grow out and then come back."

The Ammonites began to realize that they made a drastic mistake and rather than try to find a way to recover good face with David, they foolishly prepared for war.

They hired twenty thousand Aramean mercenaries and one thousand men from Maacah, the home of Absalom's mother. In addition, they hired twelve thousand men from the land of Tob.

King David called Joab to get ready for war.

As Joab went to where the enemy was gathering, he saw that there were battle lines in front of him and in back of him. So he selected some of the best troops to face the Arameans. He put the rest of the troops under the command of his brother Abishai to deploy against the Ammonites.

Joab then said to his brother, "If you see that we are in trouble in the battle, then send some troops to help me. If I see you are in any trouble, then I will send some of my troops to help you."

Joab gathered the other leaders down the line and gave them encouragement, "Be strong and let us fight bravely for our people and the cities of our God. The Lord will do what is good in his sight."

Under King David there was always a sense that the Lord was involved in all areas of living. There was a growing sense of the tie between the spiritual and the secular side of life in Israel.

At the mere advance of Joab and his troops the Arameans fled for their lives. When the Ammonites saw that the Arameans were fleeing they fled before Abishai and retreated inside the city.

Joab returned to Jerusalem. In the meantime the Arameans regrouped and decided they had been too quick to give up, especially since Joab and his troops had left the scene.

When King David was told what the Arameans were doing, he gathered all his army and crossed the Jordan River to take on the Arameans. The Arameans formed battle lines to meet David and fought against him. David and his men moved like a well-oiled machine with his troops and killed seven hundred charioteers and killed forty thousand foot soldiers. He struck down their commanders and all the remaining allies made peace with King David. In that peace they all agreed to be his subjects. The Arameans were afraid from that day forward to help the Ammonites.

CHAPTER THIRTY

By this time David had reigned in Israel for twelve years. In addition, David had ruled in Hebron seven years and David himself was now around fifty years old.

King David loved Yahweh. He believed until now, he had accomplished the will of God for himself and the Nation of Israel. From the time he had been barely a teenager, anointed by the great prophet Samuel to become king of Israel, until now, that he had established the Kingdom of Israel for the world to see. David was a passionate man and had lived and ruled with all his heart.

He worshipped God also with all his heart and had written song after song extolling the virtues of God. He was diligent in this relationship, seeking to be obedient and seeking to follow the will of God.

He loved the people of Israel. Although the people regarded him highly and followed him faithfully, oddly, something was still missing for him. Unexplainably, the personal satisfaction just was not there for David. He found it difficult to languish in the status quo.

He knew that people were fickle and there were many interests in conflict in his making decisions as their king. When some were satisfied there were always others who were not satisfied. This left David with a longing in his heart for a greater sense of personal satisfaction. The kind of personal satisfaction he desired, he found with a woman in his arms.

David had been excited to live the life of the warrior. It was with great satisfaction that he defeated his enemies and conquered new lands. He loved expanding the territories of Israel. But as he was now moving into the day-to-day maintenance of the nation, life became mundane.

In David's public life the women of Israel adored David. It was women who had made up songs all his life cherishing his bravery, success and even his beauty. So flirting and eye contact with women was a normal part of play in the king's court. Every night tens of people came to eat at the king's table. Sometimes these gatherings numbered in the hundreds.

Hushai was always on the lookout for candidates of beauty to invite. It was done discreetly and seldom did the men realize the invitation was for the beauty of their sister or daughter, as opposed to the king's interest in their own particular achievements. Hushai had been David's lifelong friend since the shepherding days of their youth. He did not think it unreasonable for David to enjoy the company of beautiful women.

David had always been honorable in his dealings with women and had never taken another man's wife, so it was a little game they played to make these evenings more interesting.

The king's palace was a marvel. After having lived in tents and caves most of his life, it was a remarkable contrast to have a home built out of cedar with enough rooms to house over twenty children, eleven wives, multiple concubines, meeting rooms for his Top Thirty, banquet rooms, porticos, and even a huge third story parapet. He could walk the parapet and look over the city and the valley below that later would be called the Kidron Valley. He had a view of olive trees on what would one day be called the Mount of Olives.

He had chosen for a neighbor Ahithophel. He had been a personal counselor and a renowned elder of Judah and a lifelong supporter of David in Judah. He lived there with several of his children and grandchildren both married and single.

One such granddaughter was named Bathsheba. She was by far the most beautiful of them all and literally one of the most beautiful in all of Israel. She had been at the king's table many times. Her husband was a soldier named Uriah. He was a mercenary from the Hittites and had lived in the north. He had been with David as a loyal soldier since the cave at Adullan. He travelled often and was one of the Top Thirty of David. Bathsheba and King David had exchanged flirting looks many times. There was a fire there that neither dared to fan openly.

About a month before springtime, Bathsheba, her husband, her grandfather, and two siblings were at dinner with the king. David arranged through Hushai to seat her two seats down the side from his head of table position.

From this angle they could easily look at each other without being obvious, although the king was becoming more brazen daily in his open regard for beautiful women. Even so, King David felt he could not be so obvious as to seat her next to him, although he longed for that.

This particular night, as the wine flowed, Bathsheba ignored him. He smiled at her every chance he got, yet she looked away quickly each time.

David said to her husband, "Uriah, how long have we been together?"

Uriah was sitting on the other side of Bathsheba so as the king looked at him he was at the same time looking at her.

Uriah responded, "I got to the cave at Adullan within three days of you getting there. I had heard you were on the run and I wanted to be at your side."

While he was speaking the king was staring at Bathsheba. She was turning crimson under his stare. Her face looked like she was sitting next to a fire. Her hands started shaking and she could neither drink nor eat.

David said, "I remember you were one of the first to show up. We have had quite a run have we not. That seems like ages ago, almost another life time."

Uriah said, "It has been a great history, Yahweh has granted you victory every step of the way."

Bathsheba quietly turned to her husband and interrupted, "My husband I am feeling very ill, almost like I will faint. Please take me home."

Uriah looked at her and then at the king, and said, "I beg forgiveness; my wife has taken ill, may we be excused so I can take her home?"

David rose and with kindness spoke quietly, "Please be excused. May I have one of my doctors help you?"

Uriah said, "No, I am sure it is not serious, just a womanly thing."

Bathsheba got out of there as fast as she could. She was ready to throw herself at the king and couldn't have helped herself if she had done so.

A few weeks passed and now it was springtime and the temperature had become very pleasant. The king's parapet overlooked Ahithophel's home which also had a parapet twenty feet below. Over the winter Bathsheba and the king had been looking at each other with increased fire in their eyes. It was with a knowing connection that did not need words. The king didn't quite understand what had happened at dinner the last time, but he did not take it the wrong way.

King David was losing some interest in going out this spring to fight those settlements that were not keeping up with their tribute. There were also those who were making agreements with others to band together to stop Israel from its expansion goals. But they were not such as would truly challenge King David's kingdom.

King David, for the first time, sent Joab and his troops to destroy the Ammonites who had built up troops over the winter and wanted to rise up again. He also sent his army to besiege the city Rabbah which had been withholding tribute.

But King David himself stayed home.

King David went out on his parapet in the early evening as he did most evenings after dinner. As he looked over at his neighbor's home, suddenly Bathsheba appeared with one of her handmaidens. A tub was brought out by two servants and water was poured into it.

The servants left and there was only Bathsheba and her handmaiden there. David watched Bathsheba slowly approach the tub of water. She let go of the wrap around her shoulders enabling David to see those treasures that he longed to see. She took off the wrap around her waist and stood in quiet beauty for minutes that seemed like seconds.

She stepped into the tub and stood longer as the water was above her knees. Her handmaiden took a cloth and rubbed her back gently as she stood there. She turned as the handmaiden took each arm and carefully and slowly stroked her. David stood in amazement at the most beautiful creature he had ever seen in his life.

David watched in fascination at the cleansing ritual of this woman who he had visually adored for many years. Before he knew it she was gone. David walked around in a sensual cloud of desire the likes of which he had not known before. He took one of his women that night to satisfy that urge, but it did not do it. He thought only one could do that as he lay tossing and turning.

David couldn't wait until tomorrow. But he did. Sure enough about the same time Bathsheba came out as before. This time there was a glance to the parapet above. But not a word was exchanged. With an upturned curl of her lips and her handmaid being in league with her, the bathing ritual took on a fresh sensuality. Each turn and each stroke maximized the exposure and created an offering of visual delights that stirred the very soul of David.

He could wait no longer and he sent Hushai to tell her to come to him the third night. She was let in through a back passage away from the eyes of the household. She came and melted in his arms. She yielded all that she was without hesitation. They were in an embrace that only oneness could satisfy.

She begged the king, "Oh my love, my king, I have dreamed of you and this moment that seemed impossible to ever happen for me, I am yours."

The king could not even reply, his actions took over and before even their clothes were taken off they had come together. But by the second and third time that night there was less frenzy and more intimacy.

They continued together nightly for weeks. Neither one of them thought of much else during this time. In the past whenever David wanted a wife or concubine he had never taken one that belonged to another.

The idyllic relationship got complicated quickly. Bathsheba missed her first time of the month. So David had to try to arrange the possibility that the impregnation could have been by her husband. In his blind desire he came up with a cover-up plan.

He sent word to Joab to send Uriah back with a report on the war. Now they already had their set messengers for such reports so Joab knew something was up. Uriah came swiftly and gave the report.

David thanked him and told him, "Why don't you go home and spend the night with your wife and then return to the field tomorrow."

Uriah went out of the palace and lay down near the steps. He slept there that night and never went home. Neither did he even speak to his wife or even let her know that he was home. He was on a mission for his general and his king and that was paramount in his life.

He felt if his fellow soldiers could not be with their wives then he should not be with his either. He was a man of honor to be sure.

The next morning Hushai came to David and said, "Uriah did not go home as you instructed. He slept on the steps to the palace all night."

David sent for Uriah who came immediately to him. David then said to him, "Haven't you been away for an extended time? Why didn't you go home?"

Uriah replied, "The Ark of God, Israel and Judah are staying in tents. Joab and my lord's armies are camped in open fields. How can I go home and eat with my family and lie with my wife? As surely as you live I will not do such a thing!"

David said, "I want you to stay one more night before you go back."

David invited Uriah to stay with him and eat. He brought out the finest of his wines and literally forced Uriah to keep drinking with him, delaying the serving of food. The two of them were laughing and sharing war stories and kept on drinking until Uriah was totally drunk.

David sent him home. But again he did not go home and slept on a mat at the staircase to the palace. Hushai reported that Uriah again did not go home. The king's frustration multiplied and he had only one alternative rather than face the charge of the theft of the wife of one of his Top Thirty.

David wrote Joab a letter instructing him to put Uriah at the lead in the fiercest battle coming up. When he is at the lead point and the battle starts, withdraw your forces a distance so that he is left on his own and will die.

So Joab put Uriah at the siege of Rabbah at the hardest point where the city had their strongest defenders. The battle began and Uriah was killed. Joab then sent a messenger reporting to David that the battle had been difficult when the men of the city came out during the siege. Some of the king's men were killed including Uriah. It was a special report due to the loss of one of the Top Thirty of David's fighting men.

David sent this message back to Joab, "The sword devours one as well as another. Press the attack against the city and destroy it."

When Bathsheba heard that her husband had been killed she mourned his death. As soon as this time of mourning was over David had her brought to his house and she became his wife. She bore him a son.

Nothing about this event in the life of David was on an impulse. It had been considered and thought out. Yes, he clearly allowed himself to get carried away. But there did come a point when he chose to have her.

Then another point when he decided he wanted her as his own. Then another point, that rather than one of his soldiers being able to accuse David of sleeping with his wife and impregnating her, he chose to murder him rather than fight him in the court of public opinion.

After nearly twenty years of success, with Yahweh enabling victory at every turn, this day marked David as having chosen sin over doing what he knew in his own heart was the right thing to do.

The consequences would follow King David the rest of his life.

CHAPTER THIRTY ONE

When word came to Bathsheba that her husband had died she went into mourning. She had loved her husband; he had been good to her. But the love and attention from the king was overwhelming. She had known of David all her life. Her grandfather followed David from the beginning, and she had chosen a man committed to following David as well.

She was with child during her mourning — the king's child at that. The king had promised to take her as his wife at the soonest "appropriate" time. She could wait and she was in love. Her grandfather "knew" what was going on, but his love for David seemed to endure and he seemed to accept the situation.

When the mourning period passed David sent for her to come and live in the palace. In due time she gave birth to the child of her adultery with David - a beautiful baby boy.

But Yahweh was displeased.

King David had made a fateful choice. In the months that had passed he still was unable to face or admit the evil he had done. He allowed his love and lust for this woman to shut down his sensitivities to sin. His heart had hardened on him. One of the worst torments a man of God can suffer is a hardness of heart, knowing something is wrong but not willing to face it.

David admitted that he had lost his ability to "hear from God." He would not recognize until later that it was the same place Saul kept finding himself when rebelling against God. His rebellion had hardened his heart. Now this sin of adultery and murder was hardening David's heart.

Yahweh gave David some time to come to his senses on his own. But as months passed there was no change. David admitted nothing and took delight in his new wife.

So God, who loved David especially, attempted another way to reach David. Since David had shut down the sensitivity of his own spirit to the Spirit of Yahweh, he was going to need a confrontation on another level to face what he had done.

God sent Nathan the prophet with these words of a parable as the king gave him permission to speak:

"There was a rich man and a poor man that lived in the same city. The rich man had many flocks and herds. The poor man had one lamb. The poor man treated his lamb as almost one of his children, living with them and eating with them.

"The rich man had a travelling visitor come to his home. The rich man wanted to kill a lamb to provide a feast for his visitor. So rather than take one of his many, he took the only lamb that the poor man had and killed him to serve his visitor."

In the telling of the story, David interrupted him in great anger and said, *"As the Lord liveth, the man that has done this thing shall surely die."*

David went on, *"He shall further restore to the poor man four times what was taken from him because he did this and had no pity."*

Nathan then said words that pierced David's heart, *"You are that man!"*

Nathan knew he had David's full attention and continued with words directly from Yahweh, *"Thus says the Lord, I anointed you king over Israel, and I delivered you out of the hands of Saul. I gave to you your master's house and wives, and I gave you the house over Israel and Judah. In fact, I would have given you virtually anything you asked of me.*

"Why have you despised my commandment to do such evil in my sight? You have killed Uriah with the sword and have taken his wife. Because of this, here are the problems you have reaped for your life: A) the sword will never depart from your house because you have despised me and taken Uriah's wife; B) I will raise up evil in your own house and someone close to you will take your wives and lie with them in the sunlight of the day. You did this in secret but I will repay openly for all of Israel to see.

David stood up and then suddenly fell on his face weeping. He said to Nathan, "I have sinned against the Lord!"

Nathan replied, "The Lord has put away this sin so that you will not die as a result of this sin."

Nathan continued, "Because this child would be a testimony to your sin and give cause for the enemies of the Lord to blaspheme the Lord, this child will die."

Soon after, The Lord struck this infant son and he became very sick. However, David refused to give up because he knew of the mercies of the Lord. So David went alone and fasted and spent the night on the ground seeking the Lord to see if He would relent and let the child live.

Seven days later the child died. The servants were fearful about how King David would react to the news. The servants were whispering among themselves and David saw this. He said to them, "Has the child died?"

They said, "Yes he has died."

David got up, washed himself and asked for food to be brought after seven days of fasting. The servants were amazed at the change and one said to the king, "How is it that you are ready to move forward after having fasted and in sorrow while the boy lived and now he is dead?"

David's response showed an understanding of life, death and God that he had never shared with anyone before. David said, "I will go to my son, but my son will not come to me!" He was speaking of eternity and life after death. In his faith, David expected to rise from the dead and live in an everlasting state and be reunited with those believers that had gone before him.

After eating, David went into the house of the Lord and prayed. As he was praying in all humility he was inspired to write this Psalm (51):

Have mercy on me, O God, according to your unfailing love; according to your great compassion blot out my transgressions.

Wash away all my iniquity and cleanse me from my sin. For I know my transgressions, and my sin is always before me.

Against you, you only, have I sinned and done what is evil in your sight, so that you are proved right when you speak and justified when you judge. Surely I was sinful at birth, sinful from the time my mother conceived me.

Surely you desire truth in the inner parts; you teach Me wisdom in the inmost place. Cleanse me with hyssop, and I will be clean; wash me, and I will be whiter than snow.

Let me hear joy and gladness; let the bones you have crushed rejoice. Hide your face from my sins and blot out all my iniquity.

Create in me a pure heart, O God, and renew a steadfast spirit within me. Do not cast me from your presence or take your Holy Spirit from me.

Restore to me the joy of your salvation and grant me a willing spirit, to sustain me. Then I will teach transgressors your ways, and sinners will turn back to you.

Save me from bloodguilt, O God, the God who saves me, and my tongue will sing of your righteousness. O Lord, open my lips, and my mouth will declare your praise.

You do not delight in sacrifice, or I would bring it; you do not take pleasure in burnt offerings.

The sacrifices of God are a broken spirit; a broken and contrite heart, O God, you will not despise.

In your good pleasure make Zion prosper; build up the walls of Jerusalem. Then there will be righteous sacrifices, whole burnt offerings to delight you; *then bulls will be offered on your altar*.

David's heart was broken. He had been blind to his own sin but now knew his failure. David saw for the first time how deceitful his own heart was. Only Yahweh could cleanse the heart of his or any man's heart. He realized he was born in sin, meaning that he, as all mankind, had a propensity to sin and without the mercy of God no man could stand before him.

As David finished singing this new Psalm of repentance and faith, he began to reflect on life further. Just then Nathan came into the tabernacle to see if he could be any help to David.

David said, "You know Nathan, I have known Yahweh all my life as the 'Most High God.' I have always known that God is above all other gods. Every battle I have waged was against a people who had their own god or gods with them. I won all these battles and have always known it has been Yahweh who has given me victory over every other people and over every other god.

 "When I was a shepherd boy on the mountains around Bethlehem and stared at the stars every night, I knew that Yahweh was the Creator. He created the universe, all people, and all creatures – I have always known that.

"But I have now found a new dimension to Yahweh. I now realize that while I let myself get carried away with Bathsheba that Yahweh is a patient and loving God. He could have just killed me and been done with it for the way I turned my back on him — but He didn't. His love is great for He loved me even though I sinned against him. I realize above all that I can only live with His salvation. I cannot save myself. He has an eternal plan and the only way to fit into that eternal plan is if He will save you and me. Then and only then can we fit in!

"Another key thing I have learned is that while Yahweh has identified himself as the God of Israel for his people and with me, David, as his king – that his motivation for this relationship is love.

"It is amazing how He patiently waited for me to realize my sin. He let months go by, giving me time to repent. When that didn't work He finally sent you Nathan to give me a story to bring me to my senses.

"The goodness of God has led me to repentance."

As they sat there quietly for a few moments — for it was a tender time with tears still streaming down David's cheeks, Nathan finally spoke just above a whisper, "David, I perceive something new about you also. The fact remains; you could have been hard-hearted and refused to acknowledge that what you did was wrong. It takes a lot for a man of your stature and position to admit that he has done wrong. Some might think that you could do whatever you want simply because you are the king.

"The turnaround of your heart shows a deep and abiding humility that pulls at the love of God. Your repentance is sincere; it has been noted in heaven, although you will suffer consequences as God has said. The good news is that He will stay at your side as you experience those consequences."

They stopped talking and began to praise God with all their hearts and minds. Joy began to replace sorrow. Peace began to replace anxiety. A sense of the matter being resolved came into the mind and heart of David. He now had a basis to move on with his life. He would trust God in the consequences and from now on, David would better understand that Yahweh is Holy. Because He is Holy He wants the people called by his name to be Holy.

David did what few have done throughout history. He accepted Nathan the prophet even though the prophet brought words of judgment. Many have killed the messenger but David did not take the words as from

Nathan, but accepted that Nathan was speaking under the inspiration of the Holy Spirit.

David put his arm around Nathan moments later and said, "Our God is an awesome God, his words are true from everlasting to everlasting."

Before leaving the Tabernacle of the Lord David wrote another Psalm (32):

> **Blessed is he whose transgressions are   forgiven, whose sins are covered.**
>
> **Blessed is the man whose sin the LORD does not count against him and in whose spirit is no deceit.**
>
> **When I kept silent, my bones wasted away through my groaning all day long.**
>
> **For day and night your hand was heavy upon me; my strength was sapped as in the heat of summer.   *Selah***
>
> **Then I acknowledged my sin to you and   did not cover up my iniquity. I said, "I will confess my transgressions to the   LORD"— and you forgave the guilt of   my sin. *Selah***
>
> **Therefore let everyone who is godly pray to you while you may be found; surely when the mighty waters rise, they will not reach him. You are my hiding place; you will protect me from trouble an surround me with songs of deliverance.   *Selah***
>
> **I will instruct you and teach you in the way you should go; I will counsel you and watch over you. Do not be like the horse or the mule, which have no understanding but must be controlled by bit and bridle or they will not come to you.**

Many are the woes of the wicked, but the LORD's unfailing love surrounds the man who trusts in him. Rejoice in the LORD and be glad, you righteous; sing, all you who are upright in heart!

Here he described the pain of ignoring sin in his life. He admitted that God had a hand on him pressing him to acknowledge his sin and he lived under the pain of holding onto his sin for many months while God kept pressing him. Finally when he faced his sin, what he had done broke his own heart.

The alternative to a broken heart is a hard heart. A hard-hearted person would defend the right to sin to the end. A hard-hearted person builds a wall for the purpose of keeping God out. A hard-hearted person would tell God, "Yes, I sinned but I am only human!" As if this was some sort of defense.

David could not ultimately go against all that he believed all his life. He believed that Yahweh was his creator and that Yahweh was over all and above all. He believed that he was accountable to God – even though he was the king and all others were accountable to him!

David chose to turn from his sin and turn to God, regardless of the consequences. He turned and humbled himself and submitted to the King of kings. David trusted that God would heal his broken heart and heal his wounds that his soul suffered.

David discovered that repentance brought a comfort to his soul as the lord forgave him his sins and now true meaning in life could be found again. David reiterates the fact in song that it is the Lord's "unfailing love" that makes life worthwhile.

David's tenderness of heart made him a new man in God. Something changed dramatically. In his own life, David was always quick to judge.

When a young man claimed he had killed Saul in a battle with the Philistines, David had him killed at that very moment. When others came and said they killed Ishbosheth, he immediately had them killed.

But to the degree he had been given a chance to repent and find forgiveness, David began to consider judgment of others in a new light. Maybe he needed to give others more time to turn from their sins?

CHAPTER THIRTY TWO

After about a year the siege at Rabbah was working. Joab got control of the water supply and the taking of this city would give David a key outpost to the east. This would secure the safety of Jerusalem further by making it very difficult for any nation to attempt to march on Jerusalem.

Joab sent word to David that the city was ready to fall and told David that he should travel to the field and be the first one in the defeated city so the claims on the city would belong to David and not to Joab.

At this same time, Bathsheba presented David with another heir. She named him Solomon, which is derived from the word Shalom, or "peace." David agreed with this name for, after all, he had found his peace with God and this son showed God's renewed acceptance of David.

David already had several sons. His oldest was Amnon born of Ahinoam of Jezreel, his second wife after Michal, and from his days on the run from Saul. His second son died in his youth and his name was Chileab, the son of Abigail. Next in succession were Absalom and Adonijah, they were the sons of Maacah. Maacah was a beautiful woman from Geshur. Both of her sons had the combined beauty of their mother and David. She also bore the only daughter of David's named in the scriptures: Tamar.

Amnon inherited the sensual appetites of his father but little else. But Absalom inherited ambition, physical beauty, and capacity for leadership from his father. Absalom was by far David's favorite. He saw many of his own qualities in Absalom and took delight every time

Absalom walked in a room as all eyes turned to him. He instantly took command, which had always been true of David himself.

Absalom resented the birthright of Amnon because he knew he was far superior and much more capable to succeed to the throne than Amnon. There were many occasions for Absalom to show off his superiority. In the contests of showing skills in horse riding, spear throwing, shooting arrows, wrestling Absalom always won.

The rivalries were not good-natured. In fact, there was dread and fear whenever they took place because Absalom made sure that everyone recognized his superiority – which he always rubbed in.

At the king's table there was always tension in the air. All eyes were on either the king or Absalom, looking for their reactions to all that was said and done. David's infatuation with his own son was not lost on anyone there. Absalom got away with what seemed like twice as much as anyone else. In fact, David had not publicly corrected Absalom as far as anyone could remember.

Every night at dinner Amnon got as close to Tamar as he could. She was a beauty of all beauties. Her hair was down her back, she was curvaceous, and had a ready smile. As innocent as she was, she gave off a sensual aura, at least in Amnon's mind.

Amnon was oblivious to guarding his position as the eldest son. He was careless and did whatever he wished at any given moment. It seemed to him as though David would live forever, so he never thought about being the heir to the throne.

Amnon had a cousin named Jonadab who was a steadfast friend as well. Of course Amnon was the crown prince, and there was always another reason to be a "friend" to the prince in the palace. In a time of peace wrangling for position and advantage was the common game played in the king's court in every kingdom. Recognition meant financial gain. Those with money always wanted to get inside the palace, and those that could help do that had a great advantage.

Amnon told Jonadab about his "crush" on Tamar. It seemed the more he talked about it the more he desired her. At first Jonadab put Amnon off saying, "Forget about her, she is your sister."

Amnon would come back in defense and remind him that she was his half-sister and this made a difference. He seemed to be gawking at her every day. He hardly talked to her for fear that he would say the wrong thing. Although he was twenty years old, he acted like a child around her. He would blush and stutter and could not find anything to say.

But his desire for her burned in his soul. It seemed to him his eyes could never see enough – he wanted to see more and more of her. His thoughts toward Tamar could never be satisfied; obsessively he wanted to live them out. He complained to Jonadab until Jonadab finally came up with a plan.

Now Jonadab was a clever and conniving kind of person. Being the nephew of the king he knew there were limitations on his personal advancement, but he was always dreaming up ways to make the most of the situation. He watched his cousin Amnon in such agony over Tamar he wanted to come up with a plan to solve this dilemma for surely there would be gain somewhere in all this for him.

He told Amnon, "You are the king's son and you don't need to live in such misery."

Amnon responded, "I love Tamar, my brother Absalom's sister, so much I can't stand the pain it causes in my heart."

Jonadab gave him a plan, "Go lay on your bed and refuse to get up claiming you are sick. When your father comes to see you, ask him to send your sister Tamar to come to you and fix you a meal in your presence and eat with her."

So Amnon did as suggested and the king came to him and he pleaded with the king to send Tamar to feed him and minister to him.

David did as Amnon requested without question and seemingly without sensing an ulterior motive. Men were regarded as superior during these times. Women were to be available to do as requested, so David had no suspicions. Tamar went to Amnon's house and she prepared cakes and drinks in his presence. But he refused to eat. Amnon then said to those in the house, "Everyone must leave immediately."

After they left he said to Tamar, "Bring the food into my chamber and serve me there that I may eat of your hand."

When she began to serve him he grabbed her arm and said, "Come lie with me, my sister?"

Tamar responded, "Don't do this, don't force me, this is against all that our faith in Yahweh stands for."

Tamar went on, "I will have to live with the shame of this the rest of my life, and everyone will think you are foolish. As the crown prince you could have any other woman you wanted."

With one last plea she said, "Just ask the king, he will give you whatever you want including me!"

She had come suspicious of why he wanted her there in the first place. She had seen him leering and lusting after her in his pitiful shyness, but she had no one to confide in. But she did come with her arguments prepared. Her pleas were based on fear of shame for both of them – but that did not work. Then she proposed the argument that if he asked the king, maybe with the time that would take, the pressure of the moment would come disappear.

Amnon was in a sensually driven, lust-filled craze which could not be satisfied with words. He had to have her. He forced her down and took her on his bed.

Surprisingly to him, but not to her, shame overcame him instantly after his physical release. He suddenly lashed out in hate and yelled at her, "Get out of my house this very moment!"

As much as he had thought he loved her to the same degree he now hated her and more. She was in tears, not only had she lost her virginity, but sending her out in shame was worse now than the act itself.

She pleaded, "There is no need to do this now, and casting me out makes it worse for me."

Amnon would not listen. He called his personal servant and said, "Put this woman out of this house, now, and lock the door after her."

She had on a garment common to the king's daughters that was worn only while they were still virgins. As she was cast out of Amnon's house, she wept uncontrollably. She put ashes on her head, and walked and stumbled forth with her hand on her head crying as she went.

Absalom saw her coming home and knew immediately what had happened. He had watched Amnon lust after his sister as it was not a secret. He tried to soften things for her and said, "It is alright because he is your brother and not some stranger. It will not be held against you, so you can still get married and things will be fine."

But Tamar felt deserted and stunned. She was in horror and could not contemplate the long range effects of the damage done.

When David heard the news he was very angry. He stormed around the palace, but he took no overt action against Amnon. It was commonly known in the king's household that he was very upset, but it was also commonly known he did nothing about it.

David's emotions were tempered somewhat by the judgments handed down to him from God through Nathan. "The sword will never leave your house." Maybe this act by Amnon fit into his punishment.

Absalom never said a word to Amnon – good or bad.

CHAPTER THIRTY THREE

T he palace intrigue went on for months. Everyone wondered if retribution would take place. Then they gossiped about Amnon being above punishment as the eldest son. Two years passed and Absalom was setting the date for when the sheep he owned would be sheared. It was a joyous time, not unlike harvest time. On the last day, all would gather and celebrate with food and drink at the passing of another good year of bounty.

Absalom invited the king and his entourage to come to the celebration. But the king said, "Absalom, I would love to come. But my entourage is over 500 people and for the burden of providing for all of them would not be fair to you."

Absalom then said, "How about Amnon? Can you send him?"

David said, "Why him?"

Absalom said, "Well, not just him, but let all the king's sons come to the feast. It will be my first chance to bless the family with the bounty I have."

David said, "Very well, I will tell them all to come to your house."

As the day of the feast got closer, Absalom took three of his key servants aside and said to them, "When Amnon gets drunk at the feast, be ready, for when I say kill him, I want you to be ready to obey me."

The servants said in fear, "But he is the son of the king!"

Absalom said, "Fear not, if I have commanded you, then what you are doing is obeying me. Be courageous and valiant and be ready to do it."

As the party went on with dancing and singing and merriment, Amnon got into the party mood. He was grabbing the ladies and sneaked off a couple times to have his way. The campfire was burning 10 feet into the air. The dancing of the women could be mesmerizing as they played their castanets and twirled in the air. Two or three at a time took turns going 'round and 'round the fire while the men shouted encouragement.

The lyres strummed and drums beat an enchanting rhythm; kissing and hugging also went on around the fire. There were about 100 people present and the servants were fair game for the single men in the crowd. But all were in fun and the evening was gay and lighthearted.

As the night went on, Absalom picked his moment when few would notice Amnon being dragged off by the servants. They took him and killed him, stabbing him brutally and with vengeance to disfigure him and his genitals — marking clearly the reason for the murder.

Word spread instantly around the party and all the sons and families sobered up and were suddenly afraid they might be next. There was so much agony and crying that fear swept the party. People fled in several directions in case Absalom was on a rampage against them all.

A messenger of David's rushed to tell the king and the first word that came was misinterpreted. It was thought that all the sons were dead. By now David had a total of nineteen sons, not including those born of his concubines. The loss was devastating to his soul. The king arose and tore his garments in anguish and fell on the ground, thinking the curse from God was coming in scope beyond anything David could have expected. The "sword" was surely on his house as Nathan had prophesied, and David did not know if he could endure the judgment.

The keeper of the watch over the City of David called out that the entourage of the sons was returning to the palace. They were all weeping and in great sadness at the division and murder in the house of David. Jonadab, always at the ready for advantage, came to the king to assure him that it was only Amnon that was dead and not all the sons.

Meanwhile, Absalom fled to his mother's land in Geshur. He was already packed and had his valuables, clothes and servants ready to go. He left in the night just moments after killing Amnon and without speaking with any of the other siblings.

Absalom lived in Geshur for the next three years. Oddly, King David longed for his son Absalom every day that he was gone. He was sorry for the loss of Amnon, but at the same time he understood it. Amnon was a victim of his own sensual appetites so David could not hate him for that. And the actions of Absalom were understandable to David, but how could he show approval of brother killing brother?

It was a quandary that crippled David's decision-making ability about how to best run his own house. He took these actions as if they were punishment for his own sin against God. If he were the one being punished, how could he take action against Absalom?

At the same time, the death of Amnon elevated Absalom's position in the line of succession. He was now the oldest surviving son. So David continued to flounder in how to handle this mess in his family. Was this all God's doing, and if so, how could David punish Absalom? It had already been almost five years since the sin against God by David and the undercurrents of murder, lust, and hate were within his household the whole time.

While Absalom lived in Geshur, his grandfather was the king and he had all the privileges of the grandson. The grandfather had been defeated by David and was paying tribute to David yearly. He began having many discussions with Absalom about David, filling his mind with ideas of taking over the kingdom from David now that Amnon was gone.

He told him how to gather and recruit people to be ready to come to his side when the time came. Although Absalom was in the king's court in Geshur it wasn't much of a court. The women were few and far between, and the court was very unsubstantial in its wealth due to the tribute paid to David.

Absalom had no way of knowing how he could come back to his father. He felt he had to wait until someone brought him a word from the king. He assumed he must pay the price – which was death – unless the king would pardon him. Getting a pardon would be no easy matter. He could not go to David and ask for one — the king could just execute him without a trial.

On the other hand, there was another way to look at it in his defense. Amnon had violated his sister and killing him was just punishment for such an act. The problem was that it should have been the king's decision to take that action not Absalom's. This frustrated Absalom greatly and he found himself unable to trust and wait for justice from the king.

CHAPTER THIRTY FOUR

King David was living a new life. While many misunderstood his reclusive lifestyle, he was in fact living his life unto Yahweh. He worshipped the Lord four times per day, sometimes for hours at a time. He would even get up at midnight every night to praise the Lord. (Psalm 16)

Keep me safe, O God, for in you I take refuge. I said to the LORD, "You are my Lord; apart from you I have no good thing." As for the saints who are in the land, they are the glorious ones in whom is all my delight.

The sorrows of those will increase who run after other gods. I will not pour out their libations of blood or take up their names on my lips.

LORD, you have assigned me my portion and my cup; you have made my lot secure. The boundary lines have fallen for me in pleasant places; surely I have a delightful inheritance.

I will praise the LORD, who counsels me; even at Night my heart instructs me. I have set the LORD always before me. Because he is at my right hand, I will not be shaken. Therefore my heart is glad and my tongue rejoices; my body also will rest secure, because you will not abandon me to the grave, nor will you let your Holy One see decay. You have made known to me the path of life; you will fill me with joy in your presence, with eternal pleasures at your right hand.

In discussion with Nathan, David proposed some new thinking. "Let's consider, Nathan that all the great leadership of Abraham and Moses focused on the actions of God and the actions of men."

He went on, "Now you and I also have that revelation of God's involvement with men and what they do on earth. But now I am beginning to see that God is looking for a "heart right relationship" between God and his people.

"God knew all along that man would fail. The possibility to sin was born into the nature of man since the Garden of Eden. But God was looking for a people who would not deny their shortcomings."

Nathan interrupted and said, "Well, He found a leader and a man of inspiration who would impact history, who understood the nature of this aspect of relationship, when He found you!"

Nathan went on, "When you finally 'realized' your sin with Bathsheba, and when you were willing to admit it and ask God to forgive you — you demonstrated the kind of heart that God is looking for in humankind. Man looks on the outward appearance but God looks on the heart.

"It is a heart that is 'soft,' that will 'break,' and above all that will 'turn back' to God and ask for forgiveness. Mankind down through the ages has demonstrated hardheartedness. In sin, many have denied they sinned, or they sin and have not cared. Others have not realized they have an obligation to God to be Holy as He is Holy. When sin does not humble us and we do not feel the need to make things right with God, then our heart is hard and deceitfully wicked."

Nathan went on, "David, I see you coming to understand the nature of living as a priest before God. In addition, I see your understanding growing, in that God is keeping you and the nation of Israel safe and that you now have identified yourself as inseparable from God."

David responded, "I acknowledge that God had given me the boundaries for the nation and that it is enough. I do not dream about conquering the world as others before have. I am preoccupied with the land promised to Abraham and Moses and securing that land only."

In Nathan's mind this revealed that David was on a life journey of understanding that he was seeking as King of Israel before the Most High God. Nathan recognized that David was expanding his view as king and adding the spiritual dimension to his role.

David meanwhile devoted his life to discover the meaning of functioning on earth as a king/priest.

On departing, Nathan encountered Ahithophel who expressed to Nathan, "I do not understand what is going on with David. Whenever I talk to him about matters of state, he hardly ever shows interest. He does not want to give time to these discussions."

Nathan was not sure how to answer Ahithophel. So he said, "I assure you that the king is well aware of matters of state. Maybe he trusts and expects his advisers to handle more of the day-to-day activities?"

Ahithophel answered, "For those who I see that are ambitious, it is frustrating to them. Others I see enjoy the peace and prosperity that is coming into their households. It is true that not only is the nation prosperous, but all the tribute paid from defeated foes keeps the treasury full and taxes low."

Meanwhile, seemingly oblivious to the frustrations of some, David sang and wrote every day. He was so prolific that very little of what he wrote survived him.

David was going through a period where he was only thinking about praising the Lord. (Psalm 8)

> **O LORD, our Lord, how majestic is your name in all the earth! You have set your glory above the heavens.**
>
> **From the lips of children and infants you Have ordained praise because of your enemies, to silence the foe and the avenger.**
>
> **When I consider your heavens, the work of your fingers, the moon and the stars, which you have set in place,**
>
> **What is man that you are mindful of him, the son of man that you care for him? You made him a little lower than the heavenly beings and crowned him with glory and honor.**
>
> **You made him ruler over the works of your hands; you put everything under his feet: all flocks and herds, and the beasts of the field, the birds of the air, and the fish of the sea, all that swim the paths of the seas.**
>
> **O LORD, our Lord, how majestic is your name in all the earth!**

He was in awe of the greatness of God as he glimpsed into the truth of the God of all the earth. "Imagine," thought David, "This great God, ruler of all the heavens and earth, loves and cares for an individual such as me!"

He paid little attention to his children, even those in the palace, let alone those who lived outside. As was typical for the time, David left the children to their mothers to raise day to day. They sat a dinner together when David was in the Palace but that was about it. His monthly meetings with the Top Thirty had slowed to quarterly meetings and even then, David showed little interest. He became more and more interested in the future.

David quit feeling guilty about his sin. He knew he was forgiven and knew he faced consequences. But he also "saw" in the future another man who would one day sit on the promised throne of David. He sensed some kind of relationship but he was not able to see whether the relationship was from his own lineage or was it a spiritual identity. After all, God promised him that his throne would endure forever. What God said was true and how God performed it was up to him. If God said this throne is the throne of David, then who ever would sit on that throne by decree from God was from David!

David envisioned and prophesied that one day:

"Here is the man whose name is the Branch, and he will branch out from his place and build the temple of the LORD. It is he who will build the temple of the LORD, and he will be clothed with majesty and will sit and rule on his throne. And he will be a priest on his throne. And there will be harmony between the two."

As King David grew older he thought more about the future of his throne — not so much about who would succeed him, rather the eternal quality of that throne. He suspected that God was going to take over his throne and that somehow God would be on that throne. He became so absorbed in these thoughts that some feared he might be delusional.

As he had been preoccupied dreaming about becoming king, now he was just as preoccupied with future generations, trying to imagine what the kingdom might look like in five hundred or a thousand years.

CHAPTER THIRTY FIVE

In his frustration, and emboldened by his talk with Ahithophel, Absalom decided to take matters into his own hands. He gathered chariots and horses and hired fifty men to run before him as each day he encamped at the Eastern Gate to the city of Jerusalem. He called out to visitors travelling from other cities, "What tribe are you from to ask the king for help in judgment?"

When they told him he would reply, "It is too bad no one has been set out by the king to help you. If only he would make me his deputy, I could help you and any other man needing help in this great nation."

If any would turn toward him to bow before him, Absalom would hug them and kiss them and offer to help in whatever matter was needed. Day in and day out, month in and month out, word travelled throughout Israel that Absalom was filling a great need in the nation. As a result Absalom stole the hearts of the men of Israel.

When Absalom turned forty he asked for and received an audience with the king. He began saying, "I pray that you will allow me to go to Hebron so that I might pay a vow to the Lord. While I was in Geshur I vowed to the Lord that if He would bring me again to Jerusalem that I would serve the Lord all my days."

The king said to him, "Go in peace." So he went to Hebron.

David did not suspect any ulterior motive. He allowed his heart to be comforted by the supposed desire of Absalom to "serve the Lord." David was, after all, giving time and space to Absalom in the hopes that his heart would turn to Yahweh on its own. David knew it was not something he could force to happen.

David had not sought the Lord's guidance about Absalom, believing that it was Absalom's responsibility to acknowledge his wrong doing. He loved Absalom and maybe if Absalom went to Hebron and truly sought the Lord, just maybe he too would find repentance in his heart. Even though it had been almost nine years since Absalom murdered Amnon, David still held out hope that repentance would come to him.

Absalom set out to Hebron with two hundred male followers and their families. Ahithophel had gone on ahead of Absalom to Hebron and put together a meeting of all the tribal elders. He told the elders of Judah that David had something wrong with him and was no longer ruling the nation. He was leaving too much to others.

Since Ahithophel had been with David from the beginning, virtually everything he said was accepted by the elders. He told them, "David is hardly ever in meetings to discuss matters of state. David spends more time with Nathan than anyone else and that this will hurt us if any of our enemies learn what is going on."

He went on to say, "Men, what I have seen of David is that he has transformed from a decisive leader on top of every need and decision to a man who seems paralyzed at every turn. It is as if the nation is ruling itself. We all know that should another enemy rise up against us, we will no longer be ready to stand up against them. We need change."

Ahithophel further complained, "Since his sin with my granddaughter was found out, he has not been the same. Oh, yes he has taken care of her, but he is not taking care of even the rest of his own household. His oldest son raped a half-sister and David did nothing about it. Then

Absalom killed Amnon for raping his sister and David has taken no action."

Ahithophel went on, "But I will tell you this, David sent for Absalom to return to Jerusalem. He came back for two years and David never even met with him. Finally, Absalom showed the courage to force David to meet with him and David kissed him but never made any decision regarding any punishment due Absalom. So Absalom took this to mean he was forgiven by David."

Ahithophel declared, "I have watched Absalom carry himself in Jerusalem for seven years now. He cares for the people as his father used to care for them. He stands at the Eastern Gate every day and ministers to the needs of the people as they come for mediation and help. Let me tell you, the people love him. He is wise beyond his years; he is handsome and has a presence about him much like his father used to have. King David has sent him to come to Hebron and I think David approves that we would crown Absalom just as we crowned David nearly thirty years ago here in Hebron. Do you all agree?"

The elders of course had been aware of the rumors surrounding the king. Ahithophel could hardly be refused as he had been in the thick of all that was going on throughout the nation. After little conversation they unanimously agreed to crown Absalom and many thought that maybe David himself expected it.

When Absalom arrived in Hebron it was turned into a procession and celebration. The musicians came out in full force with singers and dancers, and the wine flowed in a party atmosphere that was far different than the crowning of David that had taken place in Hebron. But no one cared and they were glad to honor their new king – they put on Absalom's head the original crown that had been David's years before in Hebron.

Immediately, Absalom sent spies around the nation to spread the word about the crowning of Absalom by the tribe of Judah. These spies were to rally the people among the northern ten tribes to support his kingship. The spies were spaced so that each could hear a horn blow and turn and blow for the next tribe to hear the call. Absalom carefully set up a chain of trumpeters so that when the crowning took place, "the horns would blow throughout the nation signaling a new king is crowned in Hebron."

A messenger had rushed to David with the news as it was happening and that Absalom had captured the loyalty of the people.

A change came over David immediately, and all around him took note. In a clear decisive manner David commanded, "Arise let us leave Jerusalem today. We must do it quickly before he can march here from Hebron. He will bring us much evil and he will smite the city if we are still here."

All of David's men remained completely loyal. All offered to stay and fight while David made his escape. But David commanded them to travel with him, saying that the fight was not to take place in Jerusalem at this time.

David was told that Ahithophel had left with Absalom and was a close adviser now to the rebel son. David had been so close with Ahithophel all these years that this betrayal was crushing. David felt like he lost an uncle, a confidant certainly, and someone he held closer than a brother. He took a moment, while others were packing, and went off to be alone with God and wrote these words:

If an enemy were insulting me, I could endure it; If a foe were raising himself against me, I could hide from him. But it is you, a man like myself, my companion, my close friend, with whom I once enjoyed sweet fellowship as we walked with the throng at the house of God.

Let death take my enemies by surprise; let them go down alive to the grave, for evil finds lodging among them.

But I call to God, and the LORD saves me. Evening, morning and noon I cry out in distress, and he hears my voice. He ransoms me unharmed from the battle waged against me, even though many oppose me.

God, who is enthroned forever, will hear them and afflict them men who never change their ways and have no fear of God.

My companion attacks his friends; he violates his covenant. His speech is smooth as butter, yet war is in his heart; his words are more soothing than oil, yet they are drawn swords.

Cast your cares on the LORD and he will sustain you; he will never let the righteous fall.

But you, O God, will bring down the wicked into the pit of corruption; bloodthirsty and deceitful men will not live out half their days.

But as for me, I trust in you.

The power of these words gave David the strength to go on. He left Jerusalem and his entire household went with him. He left ten of his concubines to take care of the palace for however long he would be gone. It was a large contingent leaving Jerusalem, including many men of the city and all of his soldiers who had been with him since the cave travelled with him. In addition, six hundred soldiers from Gath came to show support.

As David fled in sadness the Holy Spirit brought words into his heart:

> LORD, how many are my foes! How many rise up against me! Many are saying of me, "God will not deliver him."
> *Selah*
>
> But you are a shield around me, O LORD; you bestow glory on me and lift up my head. To the LORD I cry aloud, and he answers me from his holy hill.

David clung to the hope of the words filling his spirit.

Ittai the Gittite who was leading the men of Gath came to him and pledged, "That wherever you go we will go and whatever you need we will find."

David tried to argue with Ittai saying, "You have only been with me a short while, it is not necessary for you to risk your lives on my account."

Ittai answered the king, "As the Lord liveth, no matter what place my lord the king ends up with so will we be, whether in life or in death!"

David responded to these heartfelt words, "As you say, let's go forward now."

As the mass of people moved across the Kidron valley and marched toward the wilderness, Zadok, the priest, and all the Levites came bearing the Ark of the Lord. And Abiathar, the other priest, also stood at the gate to watch all who were with the king. But Abiathar interpreted this as the end and he began to consider what his next step should be.

David walked up to Zadok and stopped him and said, "Carry back the Ark of the Lord into the city. If I find favor in the eyes of the Lord, He will bring me again and will show me the Ark and His habitation. But if He has no delight in me, then I will let him do to me as seems good to him!"

Zadok thought that these were sounding like words of doubt and passive in nature. But he was still willing to obey this king. He had watched him become more sensitive to Yahweh than any man before him. He had heard him worship God with all of his heart. Zadok was willing to do virtually anything for David.

Suddenly a new thought occurred to David. He took Zadok aside and conspired with him, "Zadok, I want you and your son and Abiathar's son to return to Jerusalem. I will wait in the wilderness until you send word of what is going on with Absalom when he gets back to the city."

So, Zadok and Abiathar returned to Jerusalem with the Ark. As the entourage of the king went forward, there was much weeping including the weeping of the king. Someone else came up to David on the way and said, "Ahithophel is among the conspirators with Absalom."

David immediately said, "O Lord, I pray to you, turn the counsel of Ahithophel into foolishness."

Just then Hushai his longtime friend and companion came up to him to encourage him and stand with him. Hushai was humble, his coat was torn and he had dust on his head in humility. An idea came to David, "Hushai if you travel with me you will just be a burden to me. But if you return to the city and say unto Absalom, I will be your servant, O king, just as I have been your father's servant —"

Hushai stood with his mouth open, wondering what the king was getting at.

David went on, "— then maybe you can defeat the advice and counsel that Ahithophel will give to him. Now anything you hear from the king's house, you get word to Zadok and Abiathar. Their two sons will be messengers — tell them everything that you hear."

Even under the pressure of the time, a big smile came over Hushai. He said, "Great idea, I will fix my clothes, take the dust off my head and get right back to Jerusalem and do as you say!"

David's wits were about him. He was sharp as ever and the old David was in charge. He might have become passive over the last few years, but he was not passive now. He was thinking on the move and strategizing for all that could happen next.

Later that day David prayed these words,   (Psalm 5)

Lead me, O LORD, in your righteousness because of my enemies—make straight your way before me.

Not a word from their mouth can be   trusted; their heart is filled with destruction.

Their throat is an open grave; with their tongue they speak deceit.

Declare them guilty, O God! Let their intrigues be their downfall. Banish them for their many sins, for they have rebelled against you.

But let all who take refuge in you be glad; let them ever sing for joy. Spread your protection over them, that those who love your name may rejoice in you.

For surely, O LORD, you bless the righteous; you surround them with your   favor as with a shield

David believed that Yahweh could directly influence even the conversations of people while they were going on. And he prayed as if that were true. He also knew that the Lord would influence and encourage the emotions of those who called upon him to rejoice.

CHAPTER THIRTY SIX

Hushai and Absalom came into the city at almost the same time. Hushai came near to Absalom and shouted out, "God save the king, God save the king!"

Absalom stopped, turned to him and replied, "Is this the kindness that you show your lifelong friend? Why did you not go with him?"

Hushai answered, "I have followed whom the Lord has chosen and whom the people and all the men of Israel choose to be their king. I follow the man in the office."

Hushai went on, "As I was with your father, so I will serve you his son, as I have been in his presence, so I will be in your presence."

Absalom said, "So be it, you are welcome to stay." In Absalom's mind his reaction to this turn of events was in his favor. He knew how much Hushai had been a help to his father. He had always been respectful and so many times his advice had been valuable. Absalom thought, "He will be a good addition to my counselors. Other than Ahithophel, the ones close to me have no experience."

Absalom was not sure what to do next. Unlike his father, he merely got caught up with being crowned king and had not thought through any first steps. So as they walked into the palace he turned to Ahithophel and asked for his recommendations on what he should do first.

Ahithophel said, "Go unto your father's concubines that he has left here at the palace. Do it so that all the nation will hear about it and it will show that your father and you are clearly in conflict and that you are taking control of the kingdom. This will not leave any doubt in anyone's mind that the cord has been cut and that all will need to make a choice of who they will follow. After all, they will choose the one proving that he is in charge."

At the same time, in the wilderness where David was fleeing, Ziba the servant of Mephibosheth came and greeted the king. He brought much food for all the entourage of hundreds and thousands with the king. He brought donkeys to ride so the king would not need to walk either.

David asked him, "Where is your master's son?"

Ziba answered, "He is staying in Jerusalem. With all the uncertainty he is hoping that he will be the one who becomes king — in his own mind, that is his right by lineage."

David said to Ziba, "Everything that Mephibosheth has now belongs to you."

Ziba replied, "I humbly seek to find grace in your sight, my lord, O king."

Another man from the household of Saul, named Shimei, shouted as the king was going by his home, "Leave the kingdom, you bloody man, you son of devils, the Lord has taken your kingdom and given it to Absalom because you are a man of war."

Abishai came up next to the king and spoke, "Why should we allow this dead dog curse my lord the king? Let me go and take his head off."

David said, "Let him curse, who knows — perhaps the Lord told him to curse me. I am dealing with my own son who seeks to kill me. Let this man go, he means nothing to me."

David was still beloved by most of the nation. His failings had not reached many households and he was certainly a benevolent king. Many were weeping with the entourage as word spread as to what was going on. It now became obvious to all that David had not turned the kingdom over to his son. His son had crowned himself in rebellion.

Back in Jerusalem a tent was erected on the parapet for Absalom. It was the same parapet where David used to walk nightly and look over the city. There he was obviously cavorting with the women of the household and word of it got around the city. No one knew that this was part of the curse that David had received as a result of his sin with Bathsheba.

It was a critical time in the rebellion. Absalom was showing the city that he had taken over. But that was not enough. He called Ahithophel and Hushai and others to counsel him on what their next step should be.

Ahithophel spoke first, "Let me take twelve thousand men and I will go after David tonight. He will be tired and not organized. This charge will make him afraid and the people that are with him will also be afraid and will run when they see the danger at hand. I will kill the king only, and bring back the people with him in peace. We will take no retribution on any that went with him and this will motivate many to leave him and turn to you as their new king."

Absalom liked what he heard. But being in this position for the first time he was apprehensive. He wanted to hear what Hushai would say and see if he would agree to the plan.

Hushai spoke up, "The advice of Ahithophel is not the right thing to do at this time. You know your father and the mighty men that are with him. They are all very angry right now and are not unlike a bear robbed of her whelps. Your father is a man of war and he will not be lodging with the people, so to go there will be to miss him.

"He will be hiding in some pit or cave and lay a trap for some of the twelve thousand that spread out to look for him. He would most likely kill some of these followers and if he gets away, word will spread quickly that those who follow Absalom will be killed by David. This could cause defeat of your plan even before it gets started. If even a handful of men are defeated because of the bravery of your father, hearts will turn quickly back to your father."

Hushai went on, "I advise you to gather in a few days what army will go with you at this time and you go to the battle yourself. As you go, more will align themselves with you and more will gather to your side as you gain momentum. Then, when you come upon your father we will subdue him and those few that he still has with him. You will defeat not only him, but those few who are with him will be killed.

"If he gets to some city while you gather forces, then all of Israel will support you in defeating that city and tearing it down."

Absalom and all the men with him said as one, "The counsel of Hushai is better that the counsel of Ahithophel."

Not until later did anyone realize that it was the Lord who defeated the good counsel of Ahithophel, to the intent that the Lord might bring evil upon Absalom.

Hushai got to Zadok and Abiathar and told them all that had transpired. "Tell David not to lodge in the plains of the wilderness tonight, but to hurry and pass over the Jordan so that they may be protected by the river tonight, just in case they do what Ahithophel has said."

Meanwhile, Ahithophel saw that his recommendation was not going to be followed. He knew what David was capable of, perhaps better than anyone. He knew that Absalom did not have the judgment or understanding and would not last out the week in his coup.

Ahithophel also knew his own day was done. He had never gotten over what David had done to his granddaughter, Bathsheba. Even though their love ended up being pure, she would never recover from the betrayal of her husband. He blamed David for that.

Ahithophel went to his home. He spoke to his wife and got things in order. He told her how to access his finances and where they were all located. He then went to his country home and committed suicide; his shame would be too great to ever face David again.

Out in the wilderness, David took his entourage of thousands to the city of Mahanaim. Support quickly poured in from all around the country with food and water and even beds and utensils to provide for those with him.

David felt sorely oppressed. He and everyone with him were tired from the journey and fearful from the pressure of the oncoming enemy. David sat for a moment to pray right after he settled in the city. He took out his chordophone and began to play a short sweet song seeking the help of his Maker: (Psalm 43)

Vindicate me, O God, and plead my cause against an ungodly nation; rescue me from deceitful and wicked men. You are God my stronghold. Why have you rejected me? Why must I go about mourning, oppressed by the enemy? Send forth your light and your truth, let them guide me; let them bring me to your holy mountain, to the place where you dwell. Then will I go to the altar of God, to

God, my joy and my delight. I will praise you with the harp, O God, my God. Why are you downcast, O my soul? Why so disturbed within me? Put your hope in God, or I will yet praise him, my Savior and my God.

David began each of his songs acknowledging his need for help. He would sing about his enemies and the pressures, and yes, even the moments of hopelessness. But by the end of every song he would praise God. By the end of every song he would speak of the hope, trust, confidence in, worship, and or acknowledge that his salvation was in God and by God and there was salvation from no other.

In Mahanaim the word had spread fast that David was there and needed support. They came by the thousands to stand with David. He organized the troops, as he was capable of doing. He set captains of thousands and captains of hundreds. He divided his troops into three main bodies. Joab was over one third, Abishai his brother, was over another third, and Ittai the Gittite was over the last third.

David declared, "I am now ready to lead you."

But everyone there said, "No, you must not go with us, if we flee away they will not care about us. And if half of us die they will still not care. But you are worth ten thousand of us. It is better if you send us and stay here and direct from afar."

The king said, "What seems best to you, let it be."

David stood by the gate and sent all the people out to war. He further commanded Joab and Abishai, "Deal gently with the young man, Absalom."

Now this command was heard and talked about by all the people there that day.

Since the chain of command that had been with David for years had stayed with David, the forces of Absalom were no match.   David's men killed over twenty thousand men that day as the battle raged among the forests of Ephraim and the hill country. One of the key reasons why David selected this ground was because he and his leaders knew this ground. It consisted of sudden cliff drop offs, hills with much loose stone causing soldiers not familiar with the territory to stumble and fall easily.

There were briar bushes, dark forests, and surprises around every corner. David came to this land by design so that more men were killed due to the rough terrain than were killed by the sword that day. This was David's scheme and his war plans were executed at their best.

Absalom had named Amasa, inexperienced though he was, as his general. They came after David as one army while David had divided his troops into three bodies. Amasa had never been a general before so his strategy was little more than an open charge to where he thought the enemy was gathered.

They put on their open charge without any thought of proper deployment. The leaders, including Absalom, were riding on mules while the men ran in groups. Absalom was in the thick of the battle as he always thought his father had done.

As the battle raged, His head of hair, which earned him so much fame and attention got caught in a tree. He was literally hanging by his hair and could not get free. Word came to Joab and he and his armor bearers came and mutilated the rebel stabbing him many times in the heart, face and body.

Joab blew the trumpet sounding the alarm that the battle was over and his troops returned from pursuing the men following the rebel leader. They took the body of Absalom and cast him into a great pit in the woods.

A messenger came back to the city where David was waiting in the gate for word. Cushi the messenger said, "The Lord has avenged you today against all those that rose up against you."

David asked, "Is Absalom safe?"

Cushi responded, "May the enemies of my lord the king, and all who have risen up against you be as that young man." Cushi was fearful to come right out and say he was dead.

The king perceived the truth and was much moved and went to the chamber over the gate and wept crying out loud, "O Absalom, my son, my son Absalom! Would I have died for thee, O Absalom?"

David agonized because of words of promise from God (Psalm 132)

> **The Lord swore an oath to David, a sure oath that he will not revoke: "One of your own descendants I will place on your throne—If your sons keep my covenant and the statutes I teach them, then their sons will sit on your throne forever and ever**

David had been so sure that Absalom was next on the throne. He had trouble seeing which of his other seventeen sons would come forth at this stage. He had discussions with Bathsheba, who still held a special place in his heart. She had proposed that her son Solomon should follow David on the throne. She had been schooling Solomon in the ways of the king. David had to admit that of all his sons, Solomon was the only "true worshipper" of Yahweh that he saw.

But still David questioned himself. He wondered if he were somehow responsible for the failure of Absalom to come to his right mind and do the right thing?

If Absalom had simply repented for murdering his brother, David could have forgiven him. But his heart was hard and even after almost nine years, if anything, Absalom had allowed his heart to get even harder.

It was told to Joab on the road back that the king was weeping over Absalom. It was las if the victory was turned to mourning, for all were told how the king grieved for his son.

As they all returned to Mahanaim, no one could comfort the king. Finally, Joab came into his house and confronted him, "You have shamed all of us who supported you today. All of us who saved your life and the lives of your other sons and daughters are feeling guilty as if we have done something wrong!"

"It seems you love your enemies more than your friends. If you don't go out right now and speak kind words to all who risked everything for you, they will turn away from you and all the difficulties you have had in life will be as nothing compared to the way the rest of your life will go."

Harsh words to get some sense into the king. The king arose, wiped off his tears from his face, and sat in the gate and told them to spread the word the king is at the gate. David stood and encouraged all who came.

His great smile and words of comfort that the kingdom was once again in good hands settled the hearts and minds of the nation.

So word spread that the king had saved the people out of the "hand of our enemies."

"He has delivered us out of the hand of the Philistines, and now he has delivered us out of the hand of Absalom, yet no one brings him back to Jerusalem?"

People everywhere called for an entourage to go and meet the king and usher him back to Jerusalem. Just as David had waited patiently years before in Hebron for the elders to decide he was their king, so he waited now.

David knew that if he hastened back to Jerusalem, many could question whether he should still be their king or not. But if he waited and no one else stepped up to rally the nation, it would cause the elders to agree that David should be restored to kingship. This was in keeping with his history of not taking kingship or the kingdom by force.

CHAPTER THIRTY SEVEN

As David returned to Jerusalem a man named Sheba who was a Benjamite, from the house of Saul, blew a trumpet and declared, "We have no part in David, every man to his tent, O Israel."

As a result of Sheba's call, many of the men from the northern tribes started leaving David, but the men of Judah remained steadfast. Upon hearing the news of the call of Sheba, David called Amasa and said, "Assemble the men of Judah within three days and be here for your orders."

For some strange reason David wanted to measure this man appointed by Absalom to be his general. At the same time, David thought he might gather some of the men who had followed Absalom to turn back and stand with David.

Joab resented this appointment, but assumed that David had his reasons for doing it.

Amasa took longer than three days. This let David know that his son had made a poor choice to say the least. Then David said to Abishai, "Take over the assembled troops and go after Sheba quickly before he escapes. He will do us more harm than Absalom ever did if we do not stop him now."

Joab's men went with Abishai to pursue Sheba. Amasa caught up with them at Gibeon. When he came close Joab greeted him and asked him, "Are you feeling alright, you look a little sick?"

Then Joab came close as if to embrace him and with his knife he stabbed him in the fifth rib and tore out his bowels on the ground where he died. Then Joab and Abishai pursued Sheba together.

There was some confusion by the gathering troops as they saw Amasa lying on the ground dead in his own blood. They had followed "their general" who had led them to follow Absalom and now they were not sure what was going on. Was it a trap by David to kill them all? They had known that David had called Amasa to lead the troops, so they were suddenly unsure what this meant.

One of Joab's men saw the confusion and took the body and hid it to the side of the road. The men coming after paid no attention and followed Joab as if they were still doing what Amasa had called them to do.

As they marched after Sheba, more and more followers fell in line with Joab and Abishai to support David and destroy this new rebel who wanted to tear down the kingdom. They chased Sheba finally to a city called Bethmaachah. They surrounded the city and were ready to tear down the walls of the city when a wise woman cried out from the wall.

She said, "Joab, come near that I may speak to you."

He did so and the woman said, "Are you Joab?"

He answered, "I am he."

She said, "Will you listen to my words?"

He answered, "Speak forth."

She pleaded, "Do you seek to destroy a city and a mother in Israel?"

Joab responded, "Far be it from me that I should swallow up and destroy a city. I did not come to destroy the city. I came for a traitor who has lifted up his hand against the king. His name is Sheba. Deliver him only and I will depart from the city."

The woman answered, "His head shall be thrown to you over the wall."

When the head came over the wall, Joab sounded the trumpet and everyone retired from the hunt and returned to their own tents. Joab returned to Jerusalem and to the king.

Joab was once again over all the armies of Israel.

David put different people in positions around him. One key spot was given to Ira to be his chief assistant. He kept Zadok and Abiathar as priests. He put Adoram over all the tribute due from the conquered territories, Jehoshaphat was the accountant and Sheva was his secretary.

Once again the kingdom was at peace. But the calm was short-lived as a three-year famine fell upon the land.

David asked the Lord, "Why is there this famine?"

The Lord answered, "It is because of what Saul had done to the Gibeonites when he mistreated them and killed many of them for no reason."

David called the leaders of the Gibeonites to meet with him.

At the meeting David asked them, "What shall I do for you to make atonement for the sins against you by Saul, so that you may bless the inheritance of the Lord?"

They answered the king and said, "We do not want any gold or silver from Saul's house. Nor do we want you to kill anyone from his household."

David then said, "Well, what would you have me do then?"

They answered, "Let seven of Saul's heritage be delivered to us and we will hang them unto the Lord in Gibeah, Saul's hometown."

David replied, "I will give them to you."

David again spared Mephibosheth because of his oath to Jonathan. He took two sons of Aiah who was a sister of Mephibosheth and he took five sons of Michal, the daughter of Saul whom he had also married but the sons were not his. He delivered them to the Gibeonites and they hanged them on the day of the barley harvest.

Aiah stood guard over the seven sons, keeping all the vultures away and it was reported to David.

David gathered the bones of Saul, of Jonathan, and of these seven sons, and buried them respectfully in the country of Benjamin in the burial plot of the famous man Kish who was Saul's father. After that God was entreated for the land and the famine ended and the harvest became plentiful once again.

David returned to the palace and to his workshop. Whenever possible he would go back to making musical instruments. He had made well over five thousand instruments in his life time. He loved to make lyres, psalteries, and harps. They were stringed instruments. He used acacia wood and would make the instruments into different sizes and shapes. He was always listening for tone quality and became a perfectionist creating instruments that would duplicate notes.

CHAPTER THIRTY EIGHT

As soon as the famine been resolved the Philistines felt that David was getting old and maybe weak, so they decided to again invade Israel.

David was no longer the menacing warrior of old and showed weakness in the battle. He no longer used Goliath's sword as in the old days. In those days, his armor bearer would hand it to him in battle and he would swing it with such force that heads would roll off anyone in the way.

But on this occasion, in the midst of battle, he put down one enemy. As he turned to take on another his turn was too slow. Fortunately his nephew Jonathan, was right there to take down the threat.

Immediately, one of the sons of Goliath attacked David from another direction and those nearby thought David had been killed. He went down heavily, but his armor had saved him. As he was on the ground the faithful Abishai saved David and killed the giant's son.

The men gathered around David and told him to not go to war any longer with them. They would fight in his name, but as one they said, "We need you alive as our king."

Soon after this there was another battle in a place called Gob where another son of Goliath was killed. Then a battle in Gob again, and a third son of Goliath was killed. Following that a battle raged in Gath and a giant with six fingers on each hand and six toes on each foot fought against Israel and a nephew of David's slew him, so that four sons of the giant Goliath were killed by David and his servants.

Peace at last.

When David got back to Jerusalem he spent three days in the Tabernacle; Nathan came in from time to time to pray and support him. David reviewed his life and all of the highs and lows.

He wrote and sang this Psalm to his Lord recorded in 2 Samuel 22:

"The Lord is my rock, my fortress, and my savior; my God is my rock, in whom I find protection. He is my shield, the strength of my salvation, and my stronghold, my high tower, my savior, the one who saves me from violence.

I will call on the Lord, who is worthy of praise, for he saves me from my enemies. "The waves of death surrounded me; the floods of destruction swept over me.

The grave wrapped its ropes around me; death itself stared me in the face. But in my distress I cried out to the Lord; yes, I called to my God for help. He heard me from his sanctuary; my cry reached his ears.

Then the earth quaked and trembled; the foundations of the heavens shook; they quaked because of his anger.

Smoke poured from his nostrils; fierce flames leaped from his mouth; glowing coals flamed forth from him.

He opened the heavens and came down; dark storm clouds were beneath his feet. Mounted on a mighty angel, he flew, soaring on the wings of the wind.

He shrouded himself in darkness, veiling his approach with dense rain clouds. A great brightness shone before him, and bolts of lightning blazed forth. The Lord thundered from heaven; the Most High gave a mighty shout.

He shot his arrows and scattered his enemies; his lightning flashed, and they were confused.

Then at the command of the Lord, at the blast of his breath, the bottom of the sea could be seen, and the foundations of the earth were laid bare. He reached down from heaven and rescued me; he drew me out of deep waters.

He delivered me from my powerful enemies, from those who hated me and were too strong for me. They attacked me at a moment when I was weakest, but the Lord upheld me.

He led me to a place of safety; he rescued me because he delights in me. The Lord rewarded me for doing right; he compensated me because of my innocence.

For I have kept the ways of the Lord; I have not turned from my God to follow evil. For all his laws are constantly before me; I have never abandoned his principles.

I am blameless before God; I have kept myself from sin. The Lord rewarded me for doing right, because of my innocence in his sight.

To the faithful you show yourself faithful; to those with integrity you show integrity. To the pure you show yourself pure, but to the wicked you show yourself hostile. You rescue those who are humble, but your eyes are on the proud to humiliate them.

O Lord, you are my light; yes, Lord, you light up my darkness. In your strength I can crush an army;

With my God I can scale any wall.

As for God, his way is perfect. All the Lord's promises prove true. He is a shield for all who look to him for protection

For who is God except the Lord? Who but our God is a solid rock? God is my strong fortress; he has made my way safe. He makes me as surefooted as a deer, leading me safely along the mountain heights.

He prepares me for battle; he strengthens me to draw a bow of bronze. You have given me the shield of your salvation; your help has made me great.

You have made a wide path for my feet to keep them from slipping. I chased my enemies and destroyed them; I did not stop until they were conquered. I consumed them; I struck them down so they could not get up; they fell beneath my feet.

You have armed me with strength for the battle; you have subdued my enemies under my feet. You made them turn and run; I have destroyed all who hated me.

They called for help, but no one came to rescue them. They cried to the Lord, but he refused to answer them.

I ground them as fine as the dust of the earth; I swept them into the gutter like dirt.

You gave me victory over my accusers. You preserved me as the ruler over nations; people I don't even know now serve me.

Foreigners cringe before me; as soon as they hear of me, they submit. They all lose their courage and come trembling from their strongholds.

The Lord lives! Blessed be my rock! May God, the rock of my salvation, be exalted! He is the God who pays back those who harm me; he subdues the nations under me and rescues me from my enemies. You hold me safe beyond the reach of my enemies; you save me from violent opponents.

For this, O Lord, I will praise you among the nations; I will sing joyfully to your name. You give great victories to your king; you show unfailing love to your anointed, to David and all his descendants forever."

CHAPTER THIRTY NINE

D avid had studied the details of his father in the faith – Abraham. He remembered that Abraham had taken his son Isaac, as commanded by the Lord, to the very mount next to where David built his palace. It was here that God had commanded Abraham to offer his son Isaac as a sacrifice. Truly a command that was shocking to consider for any father. Without hesitation, Abraham agreed, and on this place which was called Mount Moriah at the time, an angel of the Lord stopped Abraham in the midst of his obedience. The Angel of the Lord said to Abraham, "Now the Lord knows you would obey."

David had the sense of history and if this was the first place that God called a man to come and worship him, then what better place to build the Temple of the Lord that would bring glory to God throughout all the earth.

David had walked this property and measured it thoroughly. He had dreamed in detail how this temple was to be built. Entering the Tabernacle and approaching the Ark, he would become lost in prayer and worship of the Lord. Sometimes in these moments it would seem he had lost his mind. In reality, he gained another mind from beyond his earthly bounds. David called these "ecstatic moments."

He would become oblivious to his surroundings and would gain what would later be called "words of knowledge" and "words of wisdom." He would be inspired with facts and information that he had no way of knowing on his own — but they would be accurate.

He understood what to do and when to do it with wisdom that truly was from God. From the day that the prophet Samuel had anointed him to be king, David lived with a special relationship with the Holy Spirit. The Holy Spirit within David had to be "tapped into." It seemed to David the only way he could really "tap into" the Holy Spirit was to sing unto the Lord and worship him with all his heart. When he did, bowing in all humility and reverence, it would seem as if he were enabled to walk into the same room with Yahweh.

As David sought the Lord day after day, month after month, and year after year, his relationship with the Lord grew ever closer. God gave directly to David the architectural drawings for every aspect of the temple that David so desired to build. Even though it would not be built by him but by his son, David would still organize it and plan for every detail of it.

These plans entailed every dimension and every material to be used. David became so absorbed that he was able to walk into the finished Temple in his mind and see every detail. He envisioned how the gold would be refined and worked into sheets to cover the walls, how much gold would be required to make each utensil and candlestick. He could see what shape they would be and how much they would weigh. He considered every room and every piece of furniture.

These details were years in the making and David secretly recorded every step. He showed them to no one and kept these things locked up in his workshop.

It was a joy of life for David to worship the Lord. He did his best to train others how to "enter into" the Presence of the Lord. It could only happen when one would let go of all the cares and worries of this life on earth. It was not something to "conjure up." It was not as if any man could "force God" to show Himself. But it could happen when people came together with their hearts and minds set upon God. When they worshipped him in all humility and reverence He would respond to the sincerity of the hearts that would seek him.

David was one of the few to discover that God would respond to those who diligently sought Him with all their heart and soul. David was perhaps the first to teach and show others how to create such an atmosphere that pleased the Lord.

A Psalm for Giving Thanks

Shout for joy to the LORD, all the earth. Worship the LORD with gladness; come before him with joyful songs.

Know that the LORD is God. It is He who made us, and we are his; we are his people, the sheep of his pasture.

 Enter his gates with thanksgiving and his courts with praise; give thanks to him and praise his name. For the LORD is good and his love endures forever; his faithfulness continues through all generations.

CHAPTER FORTY

O nce again, Israel was in a time of peace. Often peace is harder for some nations to deal with than war and its pressures. People seem to lose some of the disciplines of life. They become careless and one of the first aspects of life to go is the spiritual side of life. Careless people are vulnerable to the sins of the flesh.

In some areas of the nation people began to worship other gods. They were not involved in the worship services at Jerusalem and were not swept up in the worship of Yahweh. They were intrigued by the gods of those they conquered and they enjoyed performing the rituals of the conquered people.

Following the restoration of David's rule in Israel, God had forbidden the king to take a census of his available warriors. God never wanted Israel to ever depend on the arm of the flesh. He never intended Israel to say, "We don't need to bother with God, we can win this war without him."

So Israel was slipping away from God, even though the king adamantly loved and served God. The people lost interest in being so passionate with their service.

David sensed something missing in the life of the nation. He was not quite sure what it was. He was being pressed in his spirit to count the warriors available in Israel. On one hand, he felt God was inspiring him to make this count by tribe. He felt God might be punishing the people for their falling away.

On the other hand, others felt that it was Satan who was pressing David to do such a thing. They questioned if David was losing his mind or not. After all, he was known to seem disconnected from present reality at times. Some wondered whether this was because he was so spiritual or if he was in fact losing his mind.

David went to Joab and ordered him to take a count. Joab argued with him vehemently saying, "The count does not matter, you know better than I that God will give us whatever we need whenever we need it."

David forcefully prevailed over Joab and the captains that supported Joab and ordered them to start immediately and get the count done.

Nine months and twenty days later Joab returned with the count. Interestingly, the count he gave was designated in this fashion: Joab said, "King, there are eight hundred thousand men available for war in Israel and five hundred thousand warriors are available in Judah." David knew it was a meaningless number in reality, because with God you can win with few or many.

Immediately David dismissed him and fled the room himself. He was broken-hearted and felt intense shame for forcing this count to be taken. He cried out to God, "I have sinned greatly in this matter. Please Lord forgive me and take away this sin from me!"

When David got up the next morning, a prophet named Gad came to him with a "Word from the Lord."

Gad said to David, "God told me to offer you one of three things He will do in response to your sin. One, shall seven years of famine come to the land? Two, will you flee from your enemies for three months as they pursue you? Or three, will you accept three days of pestilence in the land? Let me know your decision."

David responded, "Gad, we are in a hard place. I cannot determine what is best for us. I am going to throw us into the hands of God. His mercies are great."

In answer God sent a pestilence to the land and from Dan in the north to Beersheba to the south, seventy thousand men were killed. After three days, the angel doing the killing came to the gate of Jerusalem where the Lord stopped the angel from bringing death to any of the inhabitants of Jerusalem. The Lord said, "It is enough."

The angel was standing next to the threshing floor of Araunah, who was a remaining Jebusite in Jerusalem. When Araunah and his sons saw the angel they hid in fear for their lives.

David heard the angel was there and when he saw the angel he spoke, "I am the one that has committed sin, not these people who are like sheep. Punish me and my household rather than them."

The angel did not respond to David. Just then, the prophet Gad came to him and told him, "Build an altar and offer sacrifice to the Lord at the threshing floor of Araunah."

David hurried to Araunah and wanted to buy the threshing floor. Araunah pleaded with the king, "Please take whatever you need it is all for you to do with as you see fit."

David refused, "I cannot make a sacrifice to the Lord that does not cost me anything. I must pay the fair cost for the space."

Araunah relented of course, and David bought the space and the utensils for six hundred shekels. David then proceeded by hand and with the help of others began to build a huge wooden altar.

He brought in ten oxen and cut their throats and bled them out, placing them on the altar. He poured out a wheat offering and they sang worship songs and played instruments. David offered peace offerings unto the Lord. He prayed that Yahweh would forgive him and the nation for their sins.

The Lord answered from heaven in an unusual way. As they were all in worship around the altar a sudden burst of flames came from heaven and consumed the sacrifices on the altar.

David knew this was the Lord's way of answering his prayer, so this became a special place of making sacrifices to Yahweh in the future.

There was a great fear of the Lord in David. He quit going to the Tabernacle of Moses which at this season was stationed at Gibeon, for he was afraid of the sword of the angel of the Lord. He remembered the words of the prophet that a "sword would not leave the house of David."

CHAPTER FORTY ONE

David was starting to show his age by having difficulty getting around. He was arthritic in both knees and both ankles. He grew very thin as he lost his appetite and did not feel like eating. No matter how much he was covered in blankets, he could not get warm. Hushai proposed an idea to help the king. He said, "Let's find a beautiful virgin who will cherish the king and care for him. Lying with him will keep him warm."

Those closest to the king agreed and they went on a search from one end of Israel to the other. They found a beauty named Abishag a Shunammite who was willing and wanted to come and serve the king in this way.

She loved the king and served him with all her heart. The king never went in unto her, but was comforted by her in his bed every night.

David never appeared in public during this time. He kept his daily worship time with the Lord and affairs of state more or less ran themselves.

Adonijah was the younger brother of Absalom and an apparent heir to the throne as David's eldest remaining son. He heard nothing about succession for no public announcement had been made by the king in this matter. His mother Maacah urged him to make a move to be crowned king.

Learning from his brother (although maybe not a good idea) he built chariots and gathered horsemen, and fifty men to run before him wherever he went.

As he daily put on these displays he heard nothing contrary from the king. All was quiet from the palace as he called meetings with all types of leaders. He was after all a good man. He had not joined his brother in that rebellion, so he had a good reputation.

But there were key players who would have nothing to do with Adonijah. They included Zadok, the priest; Benaiah, a key Top Thirty leader; Nathan, the prophet; Shimei and Rei and other key leaders. Importantly none of the men that had served with him starting at the cave of Adullan to this day supported Adonijah.

Adonijah decided to call a gathering in which he would offer sacrifices unto the Lord. He did not call for any to join him who had not already joined, but he did call all of his brothers except for Solomon. Abiathar, the priest, joined in to perform the sacrifice; his doubts about David had never quite left.

Nathan came to Bathsheba and asked, "Have you heard about what Adonijah is about? He is setting things up to crown himself king. Now this is what you must do to save your own life and the life of your son Solomon. Go to the king and ask him this: 'O king, did you not swear unto me that Solomon thy son shall reign after me, and he shall sit upon my throne? Then why is Adonijah crowning himself?'"

Nathan went on, "As you are doing this, I will come into the room and confirm to the king what is going on about Adonijah."

Bathsheba went immediately into the presence of the king and bowed before him. She said, "My lord, did you not swear by the Lord that assuredly Solomon will reign after you and sit upon your throne?"

She went on, "I don't know if you know it or not, but Adonijah thinks he is reigning even now and you know nothing about it. He has slain oxen and fat cattle and sheep in abundance. Abiathar the priest and Joab the captain of your host are there, but Solomon hath not been called to be there.

"The eyes of all of Israel are upon you and it is time for you to tell them who shall sit on the throne of my lord the king after you."

Bathsheba added, "It will happen that when you go to sleep with your fathers that Solomon and I will be called enemies and Adonijah will have us killed."

While she spoke Nathan came into the room and bowed before the king. Bathsheba stepped out and then Nathan said, "My lord, O king, have you said that Adonijah shall reign after you? He has gone down this day and slain oxen, fat cattle and sheep in abundance and called all the king's sons, the captains of the host, and Abiathar the priest to join him in eating and celebrating. They are singing 'God save the king.'"

Nathan turned the discussion, "Have you done this and just not mentioned it to me?"

King David spoke clearly and forcefully, "Call Bathsheba back."

She returned and in front of all, David, with a power not displayed for months announced, "As the Lord liveth, who has redeemed my soul from all distress of life, I swear by the Lord God of Israel, Solomon our son shall reign after me, and he shall sit upon my throne in my place, and we will make this happen today!"

Bathsheba was overwhelmed with tears and bowed before her husband. She saw him take charge like the days of old. This was the man she fell in love with and at last he was securing the future of her son and of the nation.

David called for Zadok, Nathan, and Benaiah and they all came into his presence. He then said to them, "Take all of my servants and everyone else in the palace, and get my own mule and put Solomon on it to ride down to Gihon. (Gihon was the place of the spring that provided all the water for Jerusalem) Blow the trumpets throughout the city and shout out, 'God save King Solomon.'"

David continued, "Then let Solomon lead the procession and all of you come back here so that he may sit upon my throne. He shall be king in my place starting today; I have appointed him to be ruler over Israel and over Judah."

All present shouted "Amen." Benaiah spoke up, "As the Lord has been with David, my lord, may He also be with Solomon and make his throne greater even that the throne of David."

Solomon was called and all the servants and all the people around the palace were called to this impromptu crowning ceremony. As they marched the people of the city shouted in joy as word spread quickly throughout the city. A great rejoicing with great shouting and singing burst forth and could be heard for miles. It almost sounded like an earthquake there was such thunderous noise.

Adonijah and his guests heard the sounds just as they were getting through eating. When Joab heard the sound of the trumpet, he said, "Why is the city in such an uproar?"

Just then Jonathan, the son of Abiathar the priest, ran in and Adonijah gave him permission to speak.

Jonathan said, "Our lord King David has made Solomon king this day over Israel. The king sent Zadok and Nathan and Benaiah and hundreds of others with him as Solomon rode the king's mule. Then they anointed Solomon king at Gihon and they have all returned rejoicing and the city is rejoicing with them. Solomon is now sitting on the throne of the king."

"That is not all. The king's servants came to bless our lord King David, and prayed that God would make the name of Solomon even better than the name of David and make even his throne better than David's throne. King David bowed himself upon his bed in agreement."

David then said, "Blessed is the Lord God of Israel who has given me one to sit on my throne this day, and even I got to see it with my own eyes!"

When Jonathan ended his report a hush fell over the group. Everyone stopped eating and drinking and not a word was to be spoken as each got up to return to his respective home.

Adonijah was filled with fear because of what Solomon might do. He rushed to the Tabernacle and seized the horns on the altar crying out, "Let King Solomon swear unto me today that he will not slay me, his servant, with the sword."

When Solomon was told this he responded, "If he will show himself a worthy man, there shall not a hair on his head fall to the ground; but if he is found wicked he shall die."

Adonijah was brought before the king. He bowed himself to Solomon, and Solomon said, "Go to your own house."

CHAPTER FORTY TWO

Solomon showed much maturity for his young age, he was almost twenty years old now. His mother had been preparing him for this time. She had secured the promise from David that Solomon would succeed him as king. Fortunately Nathan was alert and intervened when he did so that she was protected and the will of the king was preserved.

While David's health was failing he seemed to want to talk daily with Solomon. So Solomon would go into the king's bedroom mid-morning every day to sit at the king's side and hear his heart about the Kingdom of Israel. Mid-morning was the time of day that David was most alert and the meetings were life changing for Solomon. David had never spent much time with Solomon while he was growing up, yet Solomon had loved and admired David and wanted to be as great a king as David.

There was something else about Solomon that David noticed right away. When he came to visit David the first time, David asked him to join in prayer. Solomon prayed as a man in love with Yahweh.

In fact, they started every meeting in song and worship. As they did, David's strength seemed to grow and he became filled with the Spirit of God. Often in these meetings Solomon felt he was talking to God Himself. He was encouraged and really believed that God wanted him as king to succeed his father. He still called his father king; he would be king to Solomon as long as he lived.

In their first meeting together David explained to Solomon how important it was for him to build a majestic Temple to the Lord. Right after the uprising of Absalom had been put down David had begun to gather workers and materials in preparation for the building of house of the Lord. He explained to Solomon how the Lord had forbidden him from building the house of God because of the blood on his hands from so much killing.

God had promised him through Nathan that his son would build the temple and time was right to begin. David thought this was to be the major project of Solomon's reign as king.

David went on to explain how he had prepared everything. He said, "I gathered all the strangers that were living in Israel and I set the masons to hew stones in the mountains around the city. They are stored there to be brought to Mt. Zion when the building is to begin. In addition, I prepared iron in abundance for nails for the doors, and for all the joining of gates. Brass is also in abundance stored out of the city. There is enough gathered for all you will need."

David went on, "Our friends have sent us cedar wood in abundance from Zidon and from Tyre."

David spoke on a personal level now with Solomon. He began, "Solomon, I am charging you to build the most magnificent building anywhere in the world. This building must be the talk of the world and people will travel from all over to see it. Let no expense be spared. It must be grand and seen from miles away; it must shine in the sun and give glory to Yahweh."

David already had the workmen hired for all the timber and hewers of stone, and all craftsmen skilled in working with brass and silver and gold. "I have already secured the financing and all the gold you need is ready. All you need to do is arise and build!"

David then told Solomon, "God promised me a son born to me who will succeed me. You are that son. God further promised that you will be a man of rest and God will give you rest from all of our enemies. He promised you peace and quietness for all of Israel in all of your days.

"God went on with his promise to me, 'that son — and his name is Solomon — will be my son, and I will be his Father, and I will establish the throne of his kingdom over Israel forever.'"

David then called Solomon closer to him on the bed, he laid hands on his head and prayed over him, "Now my son, the Lord be with you, and prosper you, and build the house of the Lord thy God, as He has required of you. May the Lord give you wisdom and understanding, may He give you direction concerning Israel. Above all may you keep the law of the Lord thy God and then shall you prosper."

He went on in prayer, "If you will follow and fulfill the laws and statutes and the judgments which the Lord gave to Moses concerning Israel, all these things will be yours. Be strong and of good courage. Don't be afraid of anything or anyone; do not let yourself be discouraged or dismayed."

David made clear to Solomon that day that every promise of God is conditional, that God will perform his word of promise as we meet the conditions that are attached to that promise.

In the privacy of the bedroom with the two of them and Abishag, David asked of Solomon to remember a few people and Solomon pledged that he would.

"First of all, take care of Joab. He killed two captains of the armies of Israel in a time of peace. He killed Abner and he killed Amasa. Now I want you to do what you see fit, but don't let him die a natural death in peace. Now the sons of Barzillai — let them eat at your table. They were kind to me when I was fleeing from Absalom and provided food to those with me.

"Now concerning Shimei who cursed me when I was leaving Jerusalem, I promised not to kill him. But in your wisdom find a way so that he does not die living a full life in peace.

Then there was a knock on the door and the messenger said that the men David had sent for of all the tribal and key military leaders to come on this day had arrived. Now he became excited. He was filled with the Holy Spirit and got up out of bed with the help of Abishag and Solomon. He went into the great hall of the palace and a hush came over the waiting crowd.

Not many had seen the deterioration of the great king who looked quite frail and walking only with help. But somehow David made his voice heard by all and he charged them: "My time is close at hand. My last command to you is to stand with and help my son Solomon. Is not the Lord with you? You have rest from all of our enemies, and all the surrounding inhabitants are under my control. The land is subdued before the Lord and before his people.

"Now, set your heart and your soul to seek the Lord — the Lord your God. Arise from here and build the sanctuary of the Lord God and bring the Ark of the Covenant of the Lord and all the Holy vessels of God into the house that is to be built to the name of the Lord.

"The Lord forbade me to build this house, but I made plans to build it and put together all the materials needed to build it. I believed it necessary to build a place of rest for the Ark and for a footstool for our

God. But God told me I was not to build the house for His name because I was a warrior and shed much blood.

"Yet the Lord chose me to be the king over all of Israel and chose my family of Judah as leader and of my father's sons he chose me. Now of all my sons – and the Lord has given me many – He has chosen my son Solomon to sit on the throne of the kingdom of the Lord over Israel.

"He said to me, 'Solomon your son is the one who will build my house and my courts, for I have chosen him to be my son, and I will be his Father. I will establish his kingdom forever if he is unswerving in carrying out my commands and laws as it is done now.'"

David's voice found even more strength from above as he turned to Solomon in front of them all and said, "My son Solomon, acknowledge the God of your father, and serve him with wholehearted devotion and a willing mind, for the Lord searches every heart and understands every motive behind the thoughts. If you seek him, He will be found by you; but if you forsake him, He will reject you forever. Just think – the Lord has chosen you to build a temple as a sanctuary. Be strong and do the work you are called to do!"

Hushai, his faithful friend came to his side and handed David the plans. In front of everyone, David handed the documents to Solomon and said, "Here are all the plans for the portico of the temple, all the buildings, and storerooms, the upper levels, and the inner rooms, and the special place for atonement to take place. Here are plans given to me by the Holy Spirit and they further include the courts of the temple of God and for the treasuries for the dedicated things. There are also here plans how to use the priests and the Levites for service and all the articles to be used in the service. Everything down to the weight of the articles to be used, the weight of each lamp stand, the bowls, tables, dishes, the altar incense, and not a detail was left out."

Again David called out in faith, "Be strong and courageous and do the work. Do not be afraid or discouraged, for the Lord God, My God is with you. He will not fail you or forsake you and will enable all the work for the service of the temple of the Lord to be finished. The priests and Levites are ready and know what they are to do. Everyone will obey your commands!"

It now became apparent to all that the reclusiveness of the king was not because he was lost in some delusional fog, but that he was preparing the grandest building and organizing the grandest display of worship that the world had ever seen. He had written out the plans for the services and the setting up and organization of the workers and ministers in all aspects including rehearsal schedules, positioning and choreography.

David had scheduled the use of twenty four thousand Levites who were over thirty years of age. They gathered and were set to begin building the house of God. In addition, there were six thousand Levites who were set to rule over the workers. There were four thousand porters and four thousand musicians with instruments that David had made.

David had called for morning and evening prayers to be led by the Levites. They were also to prepare themselves in purity to offer all burnt sacrifices and offerings unto the Lord.

It was an amazing feat by one man. It was unheard of in the annals of history all that he planned and organized.

David seemed to get stronger the more he talked.

David made one last challenge to all that had gathered, "I have saved wealth from all of my exploits and I am giving today, on top of all the materials and the workers that I have already paid, 3,000 talents of gold and 7,000 talents of silver.*

"Who wants to join me in giving unto the Lord for the work of the temple?"

They all came willingly and gave liberally and the people rejoiced as they heard how the leaders had given so freely and wholeheartedly. They gave 5,000 talents of gold and 10,000 talents of silver as well as 18,000 talents of brass and more than 100,000 talents of iron for the building. (* See Additional Studies for conversion to today's dollars)

There was joy to overflowing throughout the assembly. Something happened that is hard to describe but David saw it immediately. He turned to Solomon and said, "Look at the faces of the people my son. Do you see how all eyes are turned to you? Do you see the joy and the lifting of the eyebrows by virtually all of them? God is right this moment magnifying you in the sight of everyone present. They do not see you as a young man any more. They see you as the King of Israel. This is God's doing."

David turned back to the people and rejoiced with them all and praised God in the presence of all those assembled by singing out:

Praise be to you, O LORD,

God of our father Israel,

from everlasting to everlasting.

Yours, O LORD, is the greatness and the

power and the glory and the majesty and

the splendor, for everything in heaven and

earth is yours.

Yours, O LORD, is the kingdom;

you are exalted as head over all.

Wealth and honor come from you;

you are the ruler of all things.

In your hands are strength and power

to exalt and give strength to all.

Now, our God, we give you thanks,

and praise your glorious name.

David went on in his testimony before all the people, while his voice was now starting to grow faint, his words were repeated by Nathan so that all could hear:

(I Chronicles 29:14-19 NIV)

"But who am I, and who are my people, that we should be able to give as generously as this? Everything comes from you, and we have given you only what comes from your hand. We are aliens and strangers in your sight, as were all our forefathers. Our days on earth are like a shadow, without hope. O LORD our God, as for all this abundance that we have provided for building you a temple for your Holy Name, it comes from your hand, and all of it belongs to you. I know, my God,

*that you test the heart and are pleased with integrity. All these things
have I given willingly and with honest intent. And now I have seen with
joy how willingly your people who are here have given to you. O LORD,
God of our fathers Abraham, Isaac and Israel, keep this desire in the
hearts of your people forever, and keep their hearts loyal to you. And
give my son Solomon the wholehearted devotion to keep your
commands, requirements and decrees and to do everything to build the
palatial structure for which I have provided."*

David then said to the whole assembly, "Praise the Lord your God." So
they all praised the Lord, the God of their fathers; they bowed low and
fell prostrate before the Lord and the King.

The next day the people gathered under the direction of the Levites and
made sacrifices to the Lord and presented burnt offerings to him; a
thousand bulls, a thousand rams, and a thousand male lambs, together
with drink offerings, and other sacrifices in abundance for all Israel.
They ate and drank with great joy in the presence of the Lord that day.

The whole gathering acknowledged Solomon son of David as their king
a second time, anointing him before the Lord to be ruler and Zadok to
be priest. So Solomon sat on the throne of the Lord as king in place of
his father David. He prospered and all Israel obeyed him. All of the
tribal leaders and all the mighty men that had followed David since the
cave of Adullan and all of David's other sons pledged their submission
to King Solomon.

The Lord highly exalted Solomon in the sight of all Israel and bestowed
on him royal splendor such as no king over Israel ever had before.

David son of Jesse was king over all Israel for forty years. He died in
old age, having enjoyed long life, wealth and honor. At the same time,

he sought the Lord as no one had before him. He served the Lord with all his heart and soul.

It could clearly be said that King David became a Priest of the nation of Israel. He made every provision for every aspect of the worship life of the nation. For the last twenty years of his rule as king he spent a majority of his time praying, singing, and worshipping Yahweh. In response, Yahweh gave David all the details of how the worship life of the nation was to be lived.

It can now be understood by all, God was not looking for a brave man, or a strong man, or a brilliant man but rather he was looking for a willing man with a tender heart to live for God at all times. And who in trying times would return to God's way.

A thousand years later, after the birth of the Church, it would be recalled by early church leaders that "David was a man after God's heart!"

Epilogue – Two Keys

In my quest to understand how David could be so favored by God above all other men on earth, I offer to the reader two key thoughts:

1) David has always had a shadow over his greatness in the minds of the Church because he committed adultery and murder. David's life gives us new insight into God's forgiveness and the freedom that brings a person. The cleansing power of God's forgiveness through repentance brings a whole new way to look at each other. If we can learn to see each other as God sees us, love will find a new foothold in the Church. In David we can verify that God not only forgives but He forgets. It is vital for the Church of Jesus Christ to learn to agree with God's assessments.

   Psalm 103:11-17 *For as the heavens are high above the earth So great is His mercy toward those who fear Him;* **as far as the east is from the west, So far has He removed our transgressions from us.** *As a father pities his children, So the LORD pities those who fear Him. For He knows our frame; He remembers that we are dust. As for man, his days are like grass; As a flower of the field, so he flourishes. For the wind passes over it, and it is gone, And its place remembers it no more. But the mercy of the LORD is from everlasting to everlasting On those who fear Him,*

   We get confused often in this life by taking ourselves and our opinions too seriously. But from God's point of view He sees our frailties and He recognizes our weaknesses and does not hold them against us. Rather He is looking for those who will admit their frailties and sins and will humble themselves and turn to Him. Those that do, He then chooses to forgive and too forget their sins.

If God did not both forgive and forget, then how could he be so willing to identify with David?

2) The mystery of the Key of David:

Rev.3: 7-13 *"To the angel of the church in Philadelphia write:* **These are the words of him who is holy and true, who holds the key of David.** *What he opens no one can shut, and what he shuts no one can open. I know your deeds. See, I have placed before you an open door that no one can shut. I know that you have little strength, yet you have kept my word and have not denied my name.*

The above scripture is a partial quote of a prophetic passage from Isaiah 22:20-23 *'Then it shall be in that day, That I will call **My servant Eliakim** the son of Hilkiah I will clothe him with your robe And strengthen him with your belt; I will commit your responsibility into his hand. He shall be a father to the inhabitants of Jerusalem And to the house of Judah. **The key of the house of David I will lay on his shoulder;** So he shall open, and no one shall shut; And he shall shut, and no one shall open. I will fasten him as a peg in a secure place, And he will become a glorious throne to his father's house.*

The wonder of the Bible is when we interpret the Bible with the Bible we find that God has wonderful ways to communicate with us. In the Isaiah reference we see that there had been a man named Eliakim that God was going to give authority to over Jerusalem and over the house of Judah. The meaning of names tells us the story behind the story. The house of Judah means the house of praise. The name Eliakim means "God sets up." So from these definitions we can understand that in the natural sense God raised up a man to take leadership over the house of praise. The authority to take over was represented by giving him the "key of David."

The Key of David gives the holder a unique authority. In the time of David this authority is pictured not merely as a key to get into some building. It can only speak to us as an authority to move through a "door" into the spiritual dimension where God resides. In our modern language we have come to think of access points into other dimensions as portals. We know these other dimensions exist but we struggle to understand the access via the portal/door.

David had the key via his life of praise and worship of the Father. But now in the Book of Revelation we are told that Jesus would take control of the" key of David" and make available to all who believe this access into the heavenly dimension. It is now Jesus who God has "set up" that has been given the key of David to lead us to life everlasting.

I pray that all would accept the challenge that none would dismiss out of hand the truth of eternal life. Only Jesus is the way, the truth, and the life. He is the only way into eternal life. He would not have suffered the suffering He endured and still endures on our behalf if there were other means or provisions to access this eternal life. You may ask how does He suffer now? The answer is when those who believe in Him suffer then He also suffers. This is the nature of the relationship He has with us.

Ephesians 2:8-10 For *by grace you have been saved through faith, and that not of yourselves; it is the gift of God, not of works, lest anyone should boast. For we are His workmanship, created in Christ Jesus for good works, which God prepared beforehand that we should walk in them.*

The word "workmanship" gives us great insight into God and (maybe very importantly into us). The word means, "that which has been made, a work, or of the works of God as Creator." This "work" has metaphorically been described as a "tapestry" or a "painting." Just as the artist creates or paints in segments likewise God works with us. When I was in high school, my school life, studies, athletics, and friends were all I knew about life. If you painted my life, at that time, these things would have filled the canvas. But now over fifty years later my high school life is a relatively minor aspect of the painting of my life. It is now down in the corner of the painting and takes a good eye to even see it.

This helps us understand that God keeps working with us. That no matter how good or how bad life may seem. Life does go on, the picture keeps morphing into new possibilities, and it is never over until it is over. Now when we consider that we are people with a Free Will then we can begin to understand that God works in us and with us and is continually working to make the "best" picture of us and our lives based on how we respond to him.

1 Cor. 13: 12 *For now we see in a mirror, dimly, but then face to face. Now I know in part, but then I shall know just as I also am known.*

David found, after his repentance from adultery and murder, a new way to interact with the eternal Presence. God the Father forgave David of his sin, and no longer held his sin against him. David responded with daily worship experiences. Designed and orchestrated by David, these worship experiences, opened to him (as it does to us), a means to connect, communicate, and grasp the Personhood of God – at least on some level in our limited present human condition.

When Jesus returns to rule and reign on the earth the scripture says;

1 John 3:1-3 *Behold what manner of love the Father has bestowed on us, that we should be called children of God! Therefore the world does*

not know us, because it did not know Him. Beloved, now we are children of God; and it has not yet been revealed what we shall be, but **we know that when He is revealed, we shall be like Him, for we shall see Him as He is**. *And everyone who has this hope in Him purifies himself, just as He is pure.*

The mother board of a computer is first designed by an engineer that creates the path for the program to follow. The engineer builds in stops and starts that are triggered by the input. This design is then miniaturized and impressed upon silicon and then the computer program becomes what was designed. This silicon becomes what we call a computer chip and then this chip responds to the input as designed by the programmer who created it.

When we see Jesus upon His return to the earth to rule and reign His Presence shall be so majestic that He will make such an impression upon us that we shall become like Him. We will be so impressed with Him that we will think and act like Him. We in fact, will fully become the image of God. When He returns it will not be humbly and lowly in a manger, but He will come in all His glory and all His majesty. His Presence will be overwhelming in greatness and grandeur. He will be the most beautiful and wonderful Presence ever seen or known by mankind. When He came the first time, He came as one of us to identify with us. When He comes again He will come as He truly is. All mankind will gladly worship Him and call upon His Holiness and Goodness. There will come a never before sense of belonging and security and purity in the hearts and minds of all who believe.

Come Lord Jesus – come!

Additional Biblical Studies concerning David

Below are some additional thoughts for further study on David – the topics are random:

True Worshippers:

John 4:21-24 *"Believe me, dear woman; the time is coming when it will no longer matter whether you worship the Father on this mountain or in Jerusalem. You Samaritans know very little about the one you worship, while we Jews know all about him, for salvation comes through the Jews. But the time is coming—indeed it's here now—when true worshipers will worship the Father in spirit and in truth. The Father is looking for those who will worship him that way. For God is Spirit, so those who worship him must worship in spirit and in truth."*

One day Jesus was waiting for His disciples and He stood by the well in Samaria. There was a woman there by herself, and they began a conversation. It was quite out of order to talk to her as by the fact she was alone gave evidence that she was a woman with a bad reputation. But it was in this conversation that Jesus chose to reveal something about the Father. Nowhere else in the Bible does it tell us what God the Father is looking for in people. Jesus declared He is looking for "true worshippers" who will worship him in spirit and truth.

Maybe this is the key to David's heart. He spent half of his kingship worshipping and leading others to worship God the Father.

Temple Preparations of the Kingdom by David-
this is a sum of the values based on today's gold and
silver prices:

National Treasury kept by David

100,000 talents of Gold

75 lbs/talent x $1500/ounce $180 Billion

1,000,000 talents of Silver

75 lbs/talent x $37/ounce $4.4 Billion

**David's Personal
Gift**

**3,000 talents of
Gold**

75 lbs./talent x $1500/ounce $5.4 Billion

7,000 talents of Silver

75 lbs./talent x $37/ounce $310 Million

Gifts by Leaders

5,000 talents of Gold

75 lbs./talent x $1500/ounce $9 Billion

10,000 talents of Silver

75 lbs./talent x $37/ounce $444 Million

TOTAL FUNDS   **$199.5 Billion**

This is the present value of the money that David bequeathed to Solomon to build the temple and finance the kingdom of Israel.

THE LINEAGE BETWEEN DAVID AND JESUS

<u>Luke 1: 32</u> *He (Jesus) will be great and will be called the Son of the Most High. The Lord God will give him the throne of his father David,*

This prophetic verse in the New Testament is speaking of Jesus and identifying the Promise by God to David as now being associated with the coming Savior who will be the One to sit on that throne forever.

<u>John 7:42</u> *Does not the Scripture say that the Christ will come from David's family and from Bethlehem, the town where David lived?"*

Imagine the heart of David being recognized by God in such a fashion that God chose to identify himself with David. Just as an adopted child takes on the name and birthright of the adoptive parents, so God chose the family of David and the throne of David to be His identity and connection to mankind.

2 Timothy 2:8 *Remember Jesus Christ, raised from the dead, descended from David.*

Acts 13: 32 - 37 *"We tell you the good news: What God promised our fathers he has fulfilled for us, their children, by raising up Jesus. As it is written in the second Psalm: "You are my Son; today I have become your Father. "'I will give you the holy and sure blessings promised to David.'*

Mat 21: *"Hosanna to the Son of David!" "Blessed is he who comes in the name of the Lord!" "Hosanna in the highest!"*

Rev 22:16 *"I, Jesus, have sent my angel to give you this testimony for the churches. I am the Root and the Offspring of David, and the bright Morning Star."*

In this the 6th last verse of the Bible Jesus chooses to identify with David as proof of Jesus' Kingship and Priesthood.

It is clear from scripture that God chose a man to be an example and a connection – despite his shortcomings – of the coming King/Priest that would rule and reign forever.

THE FAITH OF DAVID

Paul, the prolific writer of the New Testament and inspired by the Holy Spirit, is carrying the theme forward to the church that David was the kind of man that God was seeking on the earth.

Romans 4: 1 – 8

What then shall we say that Abraham, our forefather, discovered in this matter? If, in fact, Abraham was justified by works, he had something to boast about–but not before God. What does the Scripture say? "Abraham believed God and it was credited to him as righteousness."

Now when a man works, his wages are not credited to him as a gift, but as an obligation. However, to the man who does not work but trusts God who justifies the wicked, his faith is credited as righteousness. David says the same thing when he speaks of the blessedness of the man to whom God credits righteousness apart from works:

"Blessed are they whose transgressions are forgiven, whose sins are covered.

Blessed is the man whose sin the Lord will never count against him."

Here Paul writing to the Romans identifies the key to life. Abraham was a great man and the "father of faith." This great man was not great because of anything he did, but was great because he had faith that God would make up for all of his failings. God was his Savior for he could not save himself.

Paul goes on picking up with David's quote that while sin separates all men from God, that God's forgiveness of sin of those who admit their failure, will be restored. After all, when we fail don't we hope to find a way to be restored?

THE HEART OF DAVID

<u>Acts 13: 20 - 22</u>

"After this, God gave them judges until the time of Samuel the prophet. Then the people asked for a king, and he gave them Saul son of Kish, of the tribe of Benjamin, who ruled forty years. After removing Saul, he made David their king. He testified concerning him: **'I have found David son of Jesse a man after my own heart; he will do everything I want him to do.'**

Here in the Book of Acts reviewing the birth of the Church the writer defines what it has meant throughout the scripture when it has said, "David is a man after God's heart." He says that David sought out in his life to build a kingdom and worship God to foster a kingdom of priests.

DAVID WAS THE FIRST TO SEE HIS ROLE AS BOTH A KING AND A PRIEST-

In David's first twenty years as king he proved to be a Warrior King. In his last twenty years he proved to be a King Priest. He had a heart to lead the people in worship.

May the reader let the scriptures below speak to your heart slowly and with prayerful consideration. What was in David's heart that he was so intrigued with was also clearly in the heart of God.

Excerpts selected by the author from the Chapters listed to give us insight into this dual role of King/Priest as fulfilled by Jesus Christ.

<u>Hebrews 4:</u>

<u>Jesus the Great High Priest</u>

Therefore, since we have a great high priest who has gone through the heavens, Jesus the Son of God, let us hold firmly to the faith we profess. For we do not have a high priest who is unable to sympathize with our weaknesses, but we have one who has been tempted in every way, just as we are–yet was without sin. Let us then approach the throne of grace with confidence, so that we may receive mercy and find grace to help us in our time of need.

<u>Hebrews 5:</u>

Every high priest is selected from among men and is appointed to represent them in matters related to God, to offer gifts and sacrifices for sins. He is able to deal gently with those who are ignorant and are going astray, since he himself is subject to weakness. This is why he has to offer sacrifices for his own sins, as well as for the sins of the people.

No one takes this honor upon himself; he must be called by God, just as Aaron was. So Christ also did not take upon himself the glory of becoming a high priest. But God said to him,

"You are my Son; today I have become your Father.

And he says in another place,

"You are a priest forever, in the order of Melchizedek."

During the days of Jesus' life on earth, he offered up prayers and petitions with loud cries and tears to the one who could save him from death, and he was heard because of his reverent submission. Although he was a son, he learned obedience from what he suffered and, once made perfect, he became the source of eternal salvation for all who obey him and was designated by God to be high priest in the order of Melchizedek.

Hebrews 6:

Because God wanted to make the unchanging nature of his purpose very clear to the heirs of what was promised, he confirmed it with an oath. God did this so that, by two unchangeable things in which it is impossible for God to lie, we who have fled to take hold of the hope offered to us may be greatly encouraged. We have this hope as an anchor for the soul, firm and secure. It enters the inner sanctuary behind the curtain, where Jesus, who went before us, has entered on our behalf. He has become a high priest forever, in the order of Melchizedek.

Melchizedek the Priest

This Melchizedek was king of Salem and priest of God Most High. He met Abraham returning from the defeat of the kings and blessed him, and Abraham gave him a tenth of everything. First, his name means "king of righteousness"; then also, "king of Salem" means "king of peace." Without father or mother, without genealogy, without beginning of days or end of life, like the Son of God he remains a priest forever.

Just think how great he was: Even the patriarch Abraham gave him a tenth of the plunder!

Jesus Like Melchizedek

Hebrews 7:

If perfection could have been attained through the Levitical priesthood (for on the basis of it the law was given to the people), why was there still need for another priest to come–one in the order of Melchizedek, not in the order of Aaron? For when there is a change of the priesthood, there must also be a change of the law. He of whom these things are said belonged to a different tribe, and no one from that tribe has ever served at the altar. For it is clear that our Lord descended from Judah, and in regard to that tribe Moses said nothing about priests. And what we have said is even more clear if another priest like Melchizedek appears, one who has become a priest not on the basis of a regulation as to his ancestry but on the basis of the power of an indestructible life.

For it is declared: "You are a priest forever, in the order of Melchizedek."

Jesus has become the guarantee of a better covenant.

Now there have been many of those priests, since death prevented them from continuing in office; but because Jesus lives forever, he has a permanent priesthood. Therefore he is able to save completely those who come to God through him, because he always lives to intercede for them.

Such a high priest meets our need–one who is holy, blameless, pure, set apart from sinners, exalted above the heavens. Unlike the other high priests, he does not need to offer sacrifices day after day, first for his own sins, and then for the sins of the people. He sacrificed for their sins once for all when he offered himself. For the law appoints as high priests men who are weak; but the oath, which came after the law, appointed the Son, who has been made perfect forever.

Hebrews 8:

The point of what we are saying is this: We do have such a high priest, who sat down at the right hand of the throne of the Majesty in heaven, and who serves in the sanctuary, the true tabernacle set up by the Lord, not by man.

The day to come is certain and true when:

Revelation 11:

The seventh angel sounded his trumpet, and there were loud voices in heaven, which said:

"The kingdom of the world has become the kingdom of our Lord and of his Christ, and he will reign forever and ever."

May this be the new beginning for many?

D. Neal Mastruserio, M.D., LLC

(614)442-6647

Wound Care Instructions

Your tissue specimen has been sent to a laboratory for processing. You will receive a separate bill from the lab for approximately $150 for tissue processing and pathology.

1. Keep the dressing dry and site covered for 24 hours

2. If bleeding should occur, apply constant pressure for 20 minutes. If that is not effective, go to the nearest emergency room for assistance.

3. **Week 1:** Wash the wound with mild soap and water, pat dry, cleanse using diluted hydrogen peroxide (50/50 with water) and a Q-tip directly to the biopsy site/incision. Apply a thin layer of topical antibiotic ointment (If using Neosporin, only use for the first 3 days then switch to Vaseline/Aquaphor). Keep site covered with a bandage.

4. **Week 2:** Wash with soap and water, apply Vaseline or Aquaphor and keep covered with a bandage.

5. Continue Week 2 instructions until the wound has **_completely healed_**. Wounds do not heal best when exposed to air. If kept clean and covered with a bandage, the wound will heal faster and with a nicer cosmetic result.

Formation of a crust or scab over site is not desirable. Following the above instructions, will help promote better healing.

AVAILABLE NOW...

Books by Daryl T Sanders are available at www.booksbydaryl.com – or from Amazon at http://amzn.to/rufuvx - or from Faith Fellowship at Ft. Myers, Fl. http://www.ffwom.org

"Finding the POWER to Heal"

The subject of healing is complicated. The goal of this book is to show specific ways that we can find the power to heal. When we open our heart to allow God to speak to us in his word, power becomes available to meet our need. One of the ways He speaks when His word "jumps off the page to us" and goes into our heart knowing that it is true. When that happens, write it down, pray it to happen, and believe that it will.

We find our healing by faith. The problem we often face is that we feel guilty or feel failure when we think there is something wrong with our faith. If you have a sense of failure in the faith department this book is right for you.

If you have been sick an extended period of time this book can help you. We will look at several people in the Bible who were sick most of their life yet found their healing.

Prologue - Power in Attitude

Before we delve into the possibilities that abound in "Finding the Power to Heal" it is vital that we approach this search with the right attitude. The right attitude would be the one that Jesus directed us to have. As we will see throughout this book He continually challenged His disciples to have faith and use it! To use one's faith means to believe that what we seek is not only possible but we believe it will actually happen.

One day the disciples were asking Jesus to teach them to pray. Now they were not looking for a script or just words to say every time. They had been watching Jesus pray and then do miraculous things so they were obviously looking for this kind of prayer "power." They were looking for the prayers that truly changed things. They wanted to find out how to pray for the sick, cast out demons, and yes even raise the dead. They were not looking for words to say at every meeting. They were not looking for a better way to appear they were religious. They were looking for how to connect with God the Father and get direction, inspiration, and power.

The disciples had already seen in their Teacher that when He prayed He knew where to go and what to do and received the power to make it happen. When He prayed they heard Him find out what the Father wanted Him to say and when He said it everyone knew heaven was speaking through Him. They desired this interactive infilling of the Holy Spirit that is possible in prayer to lead them in life as they saw Jesus led.

Jesus is a wonderful teacher. He started off answering their question with a prayer outline. We have come to call this outline the "Lord's Prayer." Unfortunately we have made the outline a common repetitive prayer instead of understanding that it is a guideline for the things that are important to acknowledge and understand in our relationship with the Father.

Luke 11: 1-4 *Now it came to pass, as He was praying in a certain place, when He ceased, that one of His disciples said to Him, "**Lord, teach us to pray**, as John also taught his disciples." So He said to them,*

"When you pray, say: Our Father in heaven, Hallowed be Your name. Your kingdom come. Your will be done On earth as it is in heaven. Give us day by day our daily bread. And forgive us our sins, For we also forgive everyone who is indebted to us. And do not lead us into temptation, But deliver us from the evil one."

Jesus decided to answer their question of "teach us to pray," with a Four Part answer. "Part One" in learning how to pray is about keeping life in relational perspective. Let's breakdown the outline and understand what Jesus was getting at: God is our Father and His Kingdom is in the heavenly dimension at this time. His name is such a great name and is more important and carries more authority than any other name there is. Jesus is saying we should acknowledge that His kingdom is going to come to the earthly dimension so that on earth just as it currently is in heaven, His will is done in every thought, word, and deed. Jesus then tells the disciples that they should also acknowledge that their daily provisions actually do come from God.

Jesus goes on to say that they should be repentive in nature recognizing their failures and shortcomings as they go along in life. They should also be forgiving of others. They should ask that they not have to face the tests in life and that they be delivered from all that the evil one wants to bring in their life.

In Part One therefore, Jesus was teaching it is vital to have **ourselves in perspective** about who God the Father is and what our understanding should be of our relationship to Him.

Next in Part Two of the teaching the disciples to pray, Jesus shifts gears and gives them an analogy. He used an analogy about bothering a friend at midnight to make the point. This point speaks about a key understanding He knew His disciples must grasp to become effective men of prayer – **persistence**:

Luke 11: 5- 8 *Which of you shall have a friend, and go to him at midnight and say to him, 'Friend, lend me three loaves; for a friend of mine has come to me on his journey, and I have nothing to set before him'; and he will answer from within and say, 'Do not trouble me; the door is now shut, and my children are with me in bed; I cannot rise and give to you'? I say to you, though he will not rise and give to him because he is his friend, yet because of his **persistence** he will rise and give him as many as he needs.*

In making His point about **persistence** He uses an example about someone who has perhaps a legitimate excuse for not helping the person in need. Even though he has an excuse yet because the one asking keeps asking he will get up and give him whatever he needs. Here we can clearly see that Jesus is declaring that the **one asking has influence on the results by being persistent**.

Now for teaching Part Three Jesus declared in no uncertain terms the **proper attitude** to take in prayer:

Luke 11: **(9)** *"So I say to **you**, ask, and it will be given to you; seek, and **you** will find; knock, and it will be opened to **you**. (10)For **everyone** who asks receives, and he who seeks finds, and to him who knocks it will be opened.*

Here Jesus is laying out the key of the teaching. Keep perspective here. The disciples asked Jesus to teach them to pray. His response is laid out in a Four Part answer. Part One was intended to put the disciples in proper perspective that they were the lesser and God the Father the greater. So it was a relational understanding to prayer. Part Two was to inspire the disciples the need to be persistent at all times in prayer. In essence Jesus is saying that we cannot expect every word we ask for will be answered right away. There are complications and often a confluence of events that need to take place so our persistence is required to facilitate an effective prayer life.

Now here in Part Three Jesus admonishes His disciples first and all of us secondly to have an **aggressive, proactive, and relentless attitude in our prayers**. All too often people pray in a pleading way that sounds humble but is actually filled with doubt and unbelief. Jesus actually abhors doubtful prayers that sound humble but actually reveal bitterness in the soul.

On the contrary, He makes some declarations here that should encourage us all in the amount of power any one of us can have in prayer. Our prayers can change the outcome. Our prayers can influence the course of events. We can find our healing through prayer. We can find our answers to life's questions through prayer. God the Father has provided us with a platform to interact with Him and it is through prayer. Let us take Him at His word. He says if you ask it will be given to you – if you seek you will find - if you knock it will be opened to you!

Let's look into the meaning of the words as we go along here.

If you ask, the word includes such thoughts as; call for, crave, desire, or require –

Then you will receive. To receive includes the thoughts of; to bestow a gift, to grant, give to one asking, let have, to supply, furnish, necessary things to give over, deliver, to give what is asked.

If you seek, and the word includes such thoughts as; in order to find out, or by thinking, meditating, reasoning, to enquire into, to seek after, seek for, aim at, strive after, require, demand, to crave, demand something from someone.

Then you will find - to come upon, hit upon, to meet with after searching, to find a thing sought, to find by enquiry, to see, learn, discover, understand to be found i.e. to be seen, to be discovered, recognized, detected, to get knowledge of, come to know, to find out for one's self, to acquire, get, obtain, procure.

If you knock – as in knocking on a door. The idea is you are not standing around waiting or hoping the answer will just show up, but rather you are taking action with the idea of knocking on the door and keep knocking until someone answers the door and opens it.

Then it will be opened to you. Clearly He is promising results of the kind of persistent attitude that keeps knocking on a door until it is answered and opened.

In the New King James Version the word used in the answers are "will." He will answer, we will find, He will open. In the King James Version the word is translated, "shall." The meaning of this word carries a certainty of performance - is used of purpose, certainty, compulsion or necessity. In other words the meaning conveys the idea that there is no doubt. It is a certainty, He certainly will answer, we certainly will find, and He certainly will open.

Look how Jesus drives these truths home as a great Teacher that He is. In verse 9 (above) Jesus is clearly speaking specifically to his disciples that are in front of Him at the time of the teaching. But look what He does in the next verse (10); He changes the pronoun from you to the word, "everyone." So while He was teaching His disciples at the same time He is teaching all believers for all time that their prayer attitude should be just this aggressive.

Jesus is not done. In Part Four in this passage Jesus gives us a promise and understanding of our relationship again with our Heavenly Father and what **His attitude** is toward our prayers and toward us!

Luke 11: 11-13 *If a son asks for bread from any father among you, will he give him a stone? Or if he asks for a fish, will he give him a serpent instead of a fish? Or if he asks for an egg, will he offer him a scorpion? If you then, being evil, know how to give good gifts to your children, how much more will your heavenly Father give the Holy Spirit to those who ask Him!"*

Here Jesus uses the analogy of a son and a father. This analogy directs us to understand that He is making a striking example here of a relationship of love that when a son (or daughter) makes a request (prays) that the Father will not mislead, misguide, or harm in anyway the one asking. There is also, in this analogy, a key to our prayer requests that should include the Holy Spirit action.

Just think for a moment: Jesus is telling us that God is great and that we should come to Him in **humility** recognizing that all we have and are come from Him. Then He tells us that we must be **persistent** and not give up in our prayers. Then He tells us to be **bold and aggressive** and let our prayers be filled with expectation that what we ask, seek, and knock for will be answered and will be ours. Then He closes the Four Part answer with the idea that we should keep in mind that who we are praying to is one who has chosen to call Himself our Father. And therefore we can have confidence and faith that His love motivates Him to want to answer us and promises to never mislead us.

In closing the teaching Jesus tells the disciples that the Holy Spirit is a part of every answer. Later and just prior to the death and resurrection of Jesus He told His disciples why the incorporation of the Holy Spirit is so vital an aspect to our prayer life:

John 16:12 – 15 *I still have many things to say to you, but you cannot bear them now. However, when He, the Spirit of truth, has come,* **He will guide you into all truth***; for He will not speak on His own authority, but whatever He hears He will speak; and He will tell you things to come. He will glorify Me, for He will take of what is Mine and declare it to you. All things that the Father has are Mine. Therefore I said that He will take of Mine and declare it to you.*

Oh what a joy and promise we have in Christ Jesus. If you are reading this book obviously you are seeking to find out how does healing work? Maybe you need healing for yourself or for someone close to you. Maybe you need strengthening and encouragement in your ministry to pray for healing for others.

It is vital that everyone who reads this book do so with an aggressive attitude that you declare to find your answers! You are promised by Jesus that the Holy Spirit will show you what is available to you and how to tap into the power to an effective prayer life and healing power. I encourage you to declare out loud that you will – ASK – SEEK – KNOCK - that you will be relentless in your pursuit that you trust the Holy Spirit to speak to you along the way of reading this book. Believe that He will show you how to tap into the faith that is in you to find the Power to be healed.

It was never intended that we would have a passive, solemn religion in Christ Jesus. To the contrary, we serve God who has chosen the identity to be known as Father, bridging love as His motive for creating us and saving us. He desires that we would find all that He has for us in this life. We can be assured that what He has is always and forever good. In Psalms it says He thinks about each one of us every single day. And that every thought He has for us is for good.

Psalm 139: 17, 18 *How precious also are Your thoughts to me, O God! How great is the sum of them!*

If I should count them, they would be more in number than the sand; When I awake, I am still with You.

What a mighty God we serve. He is not in heaven keeping score of our daily failures. He is rooting for us, He wants the best for us, He is available to us, and His love conquers all. Therefore we can display an aggressive attitude that is bold in articulation and carries the belief that His desires for us are for even more than what we ask.

As you pray then pray in confidence. As you read this book then be confident that the Holy Spirit will guide you in the way to find your healing.

Made in the USA
Charleston, SC
04 April 2012